THE
ALTITUDE
OF PRAYER

THE

ALTITUDE

OF PRAYER

JOEL S. GOLDSMITH

EDITED BY
LORRAINE SINKLER

HARPER & ROW, PUBLISHERS

NEW YORK, EVANSTON

SAN FRANCISCO, LONDON

FIRST EDITION

Designed by Gwendolyn O. England

Library of Congress Cataloging in Publication Data

Goldsmith, Joel S   1892–1964
    The altitude of prayer.
    Includes bibliographical references.
    1. Prayer. I. Title.
BV210.2.G64   1975   248'.3   74–25685
ISBN 0–06–063171–6

Contents

· 1 ·

True Prayer, the Source
of Our Good

THE FIRST TIME that a person ever came to me for healing and asked, "Will you pray for me?" was when I knew nothing about prayer except the well-known childhood prayer, "Now I lay me down to sleep." Although not a very grown-up prayer or a deeply spiritual one, for many years it helped to put me to sleep at night. The reason for this would later become clear, after I had gained some understanding of prayer. I was going to sleep; I was going to become unconscious; I was going to enter a state in which I could not take care of myself; and by laying myself down to sleep and placing myself in God's hands, I was throwing the responsibility off myself, thus enabling me to relax in His care.

That is about as high a form of prayer as there is—not the words, but that attitude of "Father, I am going to be asleep. Anything can happen in my sleep, and I will not be around to protect myself. So now, as I lay me down to sleep, please take care

The material in this book first appeared in the form of letters sent to students of The Infinite Way throughout the world, as an aid to the revelation and unfoldment of the transcendental Consciousness through a deeper understanding of Scripture and the principles of The Infinite Way.—ED.

of me. Take over while I am out."

That attitude is a surrender, virtually saying, "I can of my own self do nothing while I am asleep, so, Father, You take over." It is the surrender of any dependence on material resources; it is throwing oneself completely on the spiritual.

Let me therefore tell you what happened when that first person asked me to pray for him. I closed my eyes and said, "Father, You know that I do not know how to pray, so what is the next step?"

Instantly, a voice came back and said, "Man cannot heal," and the whole responsibility dropped away from me. I still did not feel that I was praying and I still did not know how to pray. But you can see that I really was praying the very moment I acknowledged that I did not know how to pray.

Paul prayed much the same prayer when he said, "For we know not what we should pray for as we ought."[1] That is one of the highest forms of prayer ever conceived by man—not that the words will do anything for anyone. If, however, you have the feeling within you that you do not know how to pray, that you would not know what to pray for, that you may know what things you might humanly desire but you do not know whether or not they are good for you, you are praying.

Be careful what you pray for: you may get it! Many persons have chased butterflies and rainbows, positive that if they attained them that would be it, and then found themselves in trouble. So the more you can acknowledge, "I do not know how to pray or what to pray for. I of my own self have no wisdom that can reach God's grace," the more you bring yourself into an atmosphere of receptivity where the Father can speak within you, and when the Father utters His voice, the earth melts.

Nothing can equal the importance of the subject of prayer. Ignorance of prayer has kept the world in constant turmoil.

Every day I read of the tragedies that befall even those who pray

2

for themselves and for their families. When someone is killed in an automobile accident or stricken with some disabling or fatal disease, they ask, "What is wrong with my prayer?" or "For years I have tried to live a good life, a life of benevolence, praying regularly, and yet tragedy strikes my home just as much as it does the homes of those who do not pray. What is wrong with my prayers?"

The answer is that, regardless of how one prays, prayer never reaches God unless before the prayer a contact is actually made with God. We are in the same relationship to God as an electrical appliance is to its source of power. The appliance may be complete and in perfect working order, but until the connection with the electric current is made, it will not work. We could pray to have that appliance operate from now until the next century, and it still would not operate unless a contact were made with the electric current. Sincere though our prayers may be, they are worthless unless we have first made contact with our Source, God.

Answered prayer is available to anyone with a deep enough desire to discover the way of true prayer and to practice it. He can prove the efficacy of prayer in proportion to the devotion one puts into it.

In the earliest days of my coming into spiritual work from the business world, I discovered that if I could sit in silent contemplation and meditation, knowing nothing about prayer that uses words or thoughts, great things took place, not only in my experience but in the experience of those who sought my help. People were healed of physical and mental ills, of lack and limitation, and discords of every nature.

None of these prayers or silent meditations had anything to do with an appeal to God to heal me or anyone who came to me, nor were any of them directed at reforming or saving anyone. They were an attempt to get within myself to a place where I lost all

3

awareness of myself or any other self and became filled with an inner joy, a peace, and an inner glow. Above all, it was an inner release from fear and concern.

As we study the subject of prayer deeply, we discover that nothing that we say to God or think about God ever reaches Him. The only thing that reaches God is a stillness and a silence into which God can flow. God is not in the whirlwind; God is not in the noises of this world; God is not in the mumbo jumbo of our thoughts or words: God is in the "still small voice."[2] So, rightly understood, prayer is any attitude that opens us to receptivity to God's grace. Answered prayer comes only when there is an impartation from within to our awareness—not when something goes out *from* us to God, but when something comes *to* us from God.

OUR PURPOSE ON EARTH

Some of you have questioned why you are here on earth, and for many of you there undoubtedly seems to be no reason. Surely it is not merely to work for a living, or to go through periods of sickness, sin, or lack. Then just about the time one is old enough to have some sense and know how to live, it is time to die. That is not a good reason for having been born.

Everyone who has pondered this subject deeply has eventually come to the realization that we were born for no other purpose than to show forth God's glory. "The heavens declare the glory of God; and the firmament sheweth his handiwork."[3] We were born children of God, showing forth the life of God, the eternality and immortality of God.

The Master said, "Why callest thou me good? there is none good but one, that is, God."[4] We of ourselves are not good. We are but the instruments through which the good of the Father reaches the world, and we were born for the purpose of showing

4

forth the beauty, the grace, and the love of God—not our own virtues.

We were never born merely to work for a living. We were born to work for the joy of the work, for the showing forth of some measure of God's handiwork. We were never born to bring forth children in pain, to live by sweat and toil or by tears. We were born to be heirs of God, joint-heirs to all the heavenly riches. Why then have we missed the way? Because from infancy we were weaned away from God by not being taught how to live consciously in God. We were weaned away from God even when we were in our mother's womb, and by the time we were born, we were completely separated from God. We were taught to live in every other way except the God-way. Now, as the Master and many other spiritual teachers have revealed, we have to find our way back to conscious union with God and become reunited with Him. We cannot, however, be reunited with God because we have never really been separated from Him. It is impossible for anyone ever to become separated from God. "I and my Father are one,"[5] and that relationship of oneness cannot be broken by anyone at any time. It is impossible!

There could be no sin great enough to separate us from God. There could be no disaster, not even death, that could separate us from God, because a person cannot be separated from himself. One is one, and I and the Father constitute that one. You and the Father constitute that one—inseparable and indivisible, and "what therefore God hath joined together,"[6] no man *can* put asunder. It is not a question of "let not man put asunder."[6] It is a question of man not having the power to overrule God. It is a form of egotism to believe that man can undo God's work. That would make man greater than God. "What therefore God hath joined together" no man can put asunder, and God has joined us to Himself as His son, as the very manifested being of Himself.

5

That is an indestructible, indissoluble relationship, an unbreakable relationship. Once we know that, we are consciously one with God, and that brings the relationship into active expression.

BUILDING THE FOURTH-DIMENSIONAL CONSCIOUSNESS

Those of us on the spiritual path are building a temple, the temple of our consciousness. As human beings, we were born into a three-dimensional consciousness with our only faculties and capacities the five physical senses and the power of reason. All this applies to the human world. None of it applies in any way to the spiritual kingdom. "My kingdom," says the Master, "is not of this world."[7] *My** consciousness is not the consciousness of the three-dimensional man.

For centuries, one of the great mysteries of the religious world has been why a person can pray and pray, rarely receiving an answer to the prayer. No prayer that is uttered through the mind ever reaches the kingdom of God. That is why, when a person is advanced to the fourth-dimensional consciousness, true prayer requires no words and no thoughts. The highest form of prayer is silence.

Spiritual impartations begin to come to an individual when his Soul-faculties have been opened, or, to put it another way, when his spiritual or fourth-dimensional consciousness has been developed. Before that time, he could read or hear statements of truth, and yet he seemed to have no contact with his Source. Once the spiritual center is opened, however, a person begins to receive impartations in words, thoughts, or feelings from within—not made up in the head, but actually received through the "still small voice." He is then at-one, even if only in a measure, with his

*The word "My," capitalized, refers to God.

6

Source, with the kingdom of God within, and It begins to impart Itself to him.

The very moment that we receive an impartation from within, whether it is only a feeling or whether it thunders in the silence or comes as a very gentle whisper, we can be assured that some part of this mundane earth is beginning to dissolve, some problem is going to yield, or some discord or inharmony is going to be removed from our experience. In its place will come some grace from *My* kingdom. Remember always, "My kingdom is not of this world." The blessing that we receive is always the blessing of "My kingdom," a spiritual blessing, and we have no way at all of knowing what form it will take in this earthly experience. One thing is certain, however: it will come as a gift of God.

The Master said, "My peace I give unto you: not as the world giveth, give I unto you."[8] In the three-dimensional or material state of consciousness, the only kind of peace we can know is some additional health or supply, or a little more happiness in some form. But "My peace" is not of this world. "My peace" is something that the human mind cannot grasp. It is only when we attain some measure of that "mind . . . which was also in Christ Jesus"[9] that we know that peace. Probably none of us will receive the fullness of that mind, but in the measure that we receive it we receive spiritual peace and begin to enjoy "My kingdom," the spiritual grace of God and the blessings that only God can bestow. It is folly to try to ask what form they will take. Every individual will find them taking the form necessary to his experience at the moment.

With every word of truth that we take into our consciousness, we are building a temple of consciousness. Every sermon, every lesson we receive, every hour devoted to the study of spiritual literature, or every hour in the company of the spiritually illumined is a step in the building of that consciousness. But unless

7

we are continually submitting ourselves to God, the building of this fourth-dimensional or spiritual consciousness cannot take place.

SELFLESS PRAYER

When we reach the stage where we really are seeking God's grace, and only God's grace, true prayer becomes a closing of the eyes and an inviting of God:

Search me, God! Search my heart; search my consciousness, and if You find anything wrong, correct it. I do not care whether You reveal it to me or not, but correct it. *

We are not making any promises to God about being good; we are not pretending to God that we are some kind of angels. We are acknowledging that in our human way we have faults, but that none of these is to interfere with what must become the main theme of our life: "I must know God aright. I cannot finish this life without knowing God because I cannot finish this life without fulfilling whatever purpose God had for me in the beginning."

Many years ago, in the earliest days of my practice, I became very ill, and it seemed that my life could not be saved. One evening it became clear to me that I would pass that night. I thought that if that was the way it was to be, that was the way it would have to be. With that, I went to bed, relaxed, and thought that if that were God's plan, nothing could prevent me from going

---

*The italicized portions of this book are spontaneous meditations that came to the author during periods of uplifted consciousness and are not in any sense intended to be used as affirmations, denials, or formulas. They have been inserted in this book from time to time to serve as examples of the free flowing of the Spirit. As the reader practices the Presence, he, too, in his exalted moments, will receive ever new and fresh inspiration as the outpouring of the Spirit.—ED.

on. On the other hand, there was no power that could push me over.

Then came the word that I was about to make the transition, and with that realization, this is what sprang into my mind: "Oh, heavens, no! God, do not let it be! I have not yet done anything on earth that would even repay my mother for the birth pangs she had. My life has not been worth living, so far as adding anything to this world is concerned, or justifying my having been born. Do not let me go yet! Let me find myself; let me find my mission." And in the morning I woke up healed.

I was healed because in that moment my heart was pure. In other words, I wanted nothing for myself. I was not afraid of passing, but I knew that I had not fulfilled myself. I knew that there was no reason why I should have lived up to that time. Just to be an ordinary human being earning a living is hardly a reason to occupy space on earth, and I knew it.

As I have learned since, no one gets anything more out of life than he contributes to it, and if he is not making some contribution to the whole globe—not just to himself or to his family—all he is ever going to receive from life is the little bit of living he is getting. Really to live means to contribute; to live means to add something to the sum total of the good in the world.

PRAYER, A LISTENING ATTITUDE

When you pray, do not think that you are going to fool God. Let your prayer be, "Father, reveal Thyself." Then open those ears to hear that "still small voice," until eventually the way is opened through which it can be heard.

When you reach the fourth-dimensional consciousness, your prayers are without words or thoughts. They may be preceded by some statements of truth, just to set your own mental house in order and to give you the ability to listen, but the moment you are in the depth of prayer, there are no more words.

The whole secret of the spiritual life is in prayer, and prayer is knowing the word of God and then hearing the word of God. Prayer is the ability to receive instruction from the Father within. Keep your ear always open, as if you were listening for an inner Voice. When you live from that standpoint, no matter what you are doing out here with the mind or the body, you will find that you are always on the receiving end of instruction, protection, supply, or Grace. His grace is your sufficiency in all things. There is never any need for you to have anything else from God, just His grace.

Spiritual power comes into your experience when you understand the true meaning of prayer. As a person, you have no spiritual power of your own. You are but the transparency, the instrument through which the power of God flows to the world and to the people of the world.

Only in the degree in which a person can unite himself with the Source of life, the creative Principle of this universe, only in that degree can healing power, comforting power, and supplying power flow through his consciousness. The mode or means of reuniting with the Source or of attaining that contact, we call prayer.

Keep the word of God in your mouth; keep it in your mind, in your heart, and in your soul, and then pray, "Father, You take over. Now I lay me down to sleep, and I am not going to take thought any more for what I shall eat or drink. I am going to rest in Your arms. I in You, and You in me."

10

· 2 ·

Creating a Vacuum
for the Inflow of the Spirit

PRAYER CAN NEVER BE ANSWERED unless there is a fitting preparation for prayer and unless the terms of prayer have been fulfilled. And there are terms. One of the terms is humility. Humility is the particular quality that admits God into our experience. True, as we develop spiritually, other qualities can make us more receptive and responsive to God, but one of the first qualities we must acquire is humility.

TRUE HUMILITY

Humanly our lives have been lived as if we of our own selves could accomplish wonders, as if we were sufficient unto ourselves, with all the wisdom, power, and strength necessary to go out and make or break this world. Too many of us have grown up with too much confidence and faith in our own powers and wisdom, and it is in this respect that the quality of humility must be developed in us.

True humility is not self-depreciation, nor is it building an escape mechanism because of a faith in some unknown God or some unknown power. True humility understands that in the

11

beginning God incarnated Itself* as our very being. God has imparted to us Its* own nature and qualities. If we are loving, it is because there is a spark of God-love in us. If we are wise, it is because there is a spark of the infinite Wisdom in us. If we are well, it is because there is a spark of the divine Being in us.

To understand our dependence upon the Infinite Invisible is the sense of humility that I ask you to ponder. It is not that you are less than another; it is not the sense of humility that bows down before some other human being: it is the humility that acknowledges a divine Grace, a divine Power, a supreme Being in operation.

There is nothing of an enduring nature that man needs to pray for or about. That which is always has been, is now, and forever will be. Our praying will not bring it to pass one minute sooner than its time, nor would our cursing hold it back. That which God is doing God has been doing, and God ever will be doing, and praying will not change it.

Is there, then, no reason for prayer? Indeed there is, for prayer is the very bread of life. Prayer brings the Divine into our individual experience. Prayer is not supplication; prayer is not asking God to do something for us. When we understand the nature of God as eternal, infinitely intelligent Being, we will then learn that there is no use trying to influence God in our behalf, in our neighbor's behalf, or in our friend's or relative's behalf.

In the days before the telephone, fast automobiles, and airplanes, if people were taken very ill, sometimes unto death, often

*In the spiritual literature of the world, the varying concepts of God are indicated by the use of such words as "Father," "Mother," "Soul," "Spirit," "Principle," "Love," or "Life." Therefore, in this book, the author has used the pronouns "He" and "It," or "Himself" and "Itself," interchangeably in referring to God. —ED.

they passed on because there was no way to get immediate help by rushing a doctor to them or rushing them to a well-equipped hospital. Suddenly this has changed, and today we read of people at the point of death being transported from one country to another a thousand or ten thousand miles away and being saved. Life expectancy has increased because of greater medical knowledge and its greater availability.

We may wonder, "Why didn't God do that for the last generation or the one before?" It is not that God's will has changed toward us. God's will was the same then as it is now, but God was not responding any more to those frantic appeals then than God is now. Obviously God had nothing to do with it then and God has nothing to do with it now. God enters our experience only when we learn to conform to the spiritual laws of life.

True humility is an acknowledgment that God is the wisdom, the intelligence, and the love of this universe. True prayer is a coming into an at-oneness with God through this realization, not resisting the particular evil that confronts us, the lack, limitation, or pain, which may be the immediate problem, but turning from it to what we now know of God, and then enlarging our vision of what God is.

When we think of going to God to get something, we are in trade; we are bargaining, begging, pleading, or accusing. But to go to God seeking only His grace is to know that "the Lord is my shepherd; I shall not want. . . . He leadeth me beside the still waters."[1] There is no praying to God to do something, no begging, no pleading, just the realization, "He leadeth me." That is resting in Him. That is dwelling "in the secret place of the most High."[2] In this sense of humility Something is overshadowing us, a Something greater than ourselves.

13

EMPTYING OUT THE OLD

Before prayer can become answered prayer, the old vessels must be emptied. We cannot fill a vessel already full; we cannot add fresh water to a bottle of stale water; and we cannot add the truth about prayer to our former concepts of prayer.

If our prayers have not been answered, let us have the humility to begin to discard all that we have ever known and take the attitude, "I do not know how to pray. Father, instruct me." No progress will be made until we have completely emptied out all ideas of what we believe prayer to be.

When we are instructed by the Father, the first lesson we learn is that we are never to pray for food, clothing, housing, health, transportation, marriage, divorce, or companionship. We are never to pray for anything of a material nature. When we go to God in the Spirit and for the Spirit, for spiritual realization, spiritual grace, spiritual wisdom, and spiritual guidance, we will reap life everlasting, harmonious and abundant.

The moment that we seek anything of a material nature from God, we are throwing dust in the face of God, for we are saying, "Father, listen to me. I will tell You what I need that You do not know about. Let me tell You some of Your business. Let me tell You something about this world that You do not know. Let me assure You that my wisdom is greater than Your wisdom, so let me tell You what we need here on earth."

Is it possible to believe that there is a God who sits up in heaven holding back our good, waiting for us to beg, plead, or sacrifice, and then does not give it to us in the end? The answer must be clear to every thinking person: there is no such God. No God is withholding from us what is rightfully ours. No God has the power to give us the things that we believe are rightfully ours. If anything

14

is missing from our life, it is not because God is withholding it: we are setting up a barrier that keeps it from coming into manifestation.

God is not here to fulfill your desires or mine; God does not exist to please you or me. Under no circumstances does God do anything primarily for you or for me, and there is no way of compelling God to do for you, for me, for mine, or for yours. The only correct approach to prayer and meditation is "not as I will, but as thou wilt,"[3] not "Do for me what I wish done," but "Prepare me to fulfill Thy will. Let Thy Spirit be in me that I may be Thy child, that I may be one with Thee, that I may dwell in Thy house, and that Thou mayest dwell in me." God is not our servant, but it is fitting that we be servants of God. God is not the son of man: it would be well if the son of man could be the son of God.

In every case in our prayer and in our meditation, we must yield ourselves—our will and our desires—to God, and let God fulfill His will and His grace in us. Unfortunately, many have been taught from infancy that God's will is sometimes evil and that sometimes God visits sickness on His children. It is even believed by some that God causes death. If a person believed this, how could he trust himself to God, not knowing but that God may decide to strike him down in this next minute?

Jesus taught two thousand years ago that we can trust the Lord our God, that God's will is that man live, that he never know disease, accidents, or punishment for sin. In surrendering our will to God, we are surrendering ourselves to life eternal, to immortal spiritual life, perfect life, harmonious life. It is not a question of ill health or good health, but of spiritual immortality.

An Understanding of God's Nature Is Necessary for Prayer

When we surrender ourselves to God, there is no poverty and no wealth: there is the infinite abundance of allness, not a little corner of it—all. This can come about only if we perceive the nature of God as God was revealed two thousand years ago by the Master.

How can we love a God we believe is withholding, but is going to give us what we ask for after we hound Him hard enough or long enough? There is no God to withhold anything from us, and there is no God to give us anything. God is the same yesterday, today, and forever; God is the same from everlasting to everlasting. All that God is doing today, God has been doing always, and will always continue to do because the nature of God is *Is*. God is— not God was, and not God will be: *God is*. It is as if we were to say that the sunshine is. We do not pray for it to come in. We open the windows and the shades, and *let* it in.

God does not know if we need an automobile or a new house. No, God knows our need as the sunshine knows the need of the earth. The sun knows that it must shine, and God knows that God must be God. God is fulfillment. When we have the sun, we have light and warmth, for the sun is light and warmth. We do not need food, clothing, housing, and transportation: we need God, and in having God, we find that God is the health of our countenance. God is the bread and the meat and the wine and the water.

Every time we go to God with some need or desire that we want fulfilled, we have set up the barrier that keeps it from us. There can be only one way to go to God: "Thy will be done in me. Thy will be done in me that I may be one with Thee, that there be no barrier within me hiding Thy light."

16

If God could construct this universe, how much greater Its wisdom must be than ours! We could not hope to emulate that, and the universe is the very least of God's creating. God has formed us in His own image and likeness, and then we look up and tell God what He has omitted from us. No! It will not do! There will be no answered prayer unless our prayer is to a God of omniscience, all-wisdom, and all-intelligence, so that when we pray we can say, "God, cut my tongue out if I try to advise You. Let my prayer be with the ears, not with the tongue. Let my prayer be listening, not speaking."

The mind of man will never reach God in prayer unless the mind is still so that it can be receptive to the "still small voice"[4]: "Speak, Lord; for thy servant heareth"[5]—not "Thy servant is telling Thee," not "Thy servant is asking Thee." Let prayer be a listening attitude, a receptive state of consciousness, with a desire only that what we hear will transform and renew us, that every word we hear will purify and make us fit receptacles for the divine inflow.

We are the temple of the living God only when we let God live our lives, not when we try to take over and live them. We are "the temple of God"[6] when our prayer is listening, when our attitude is receptivity, when our willingness is to be purified, to be cleansed, and to do the will of the Father.

In this inner emptiness, which we have created through pondering the nature of God and the nature of prayer, we become instruments, and then into our consciousness God pours wisdom and love. It was not absent; it never is. But when we are a vessel already full, full of longings and desires and hopes and ambitions, we are not empty enough to receive God's grace. Only when we are a state of emptiness can we receive the Grace which is already established within us.

17

The Ever-Presence of Grace

Grace is not something given to one individual and withheld from another. Grace is not something anyone earns or deserves. Grace is God's gift established within each and every one of us, which we receive when we are empty.

The grace of God is not something that God can bestow upon us tomorrow. The grace of God was bestowed upon us in the beginning when we were created in His image and likeness. It is as much a part of us as our integrity, loyalty, and fidelity, and we had 100 percent of those in the beginning, and still have. Even though we may not be expressing all of them now, they are there within us 100 percent, just as they were within the thief on the cross. He had 100 percent of integrity within him even while he was committing his crimes, but he was not sufficiently empty to let God's grace and God's purification flow.

Divine Grace is more than a word. Divine Grace is a power, and It is not something for which we wait. The moment we relinquish a material faith, divine Grace takes over. We begin with "Nevermore let me pray for anything. My heavenly Father is the divine wisdom which founded this universe and maintains and sustains it. My heavenly Father is the infinite intelligence which knows the need even of the sparrow. Furthermore, my heavenly Father is divine love. It is His good pleasure to stock the seas with fish, fill the air with birds, the trees with fruit, the bushes with flowers, and the ground with grass." Do we pray for those things? No, they are the naturalness of God unfolding, disclosing, and revealing Itself to our awareness, and when we pray to make them happen, we separate ourselves from them.

God's grace is established within us. To think otherwise would

18

be a sin, because if every individual who ever has been, is now, or ever will be lacks any of God's grace, it must be God's fault. What a terrible indictment that would be to hold against the God of wisdom and the God of love! God's grace is within us. "The kingdom of God is within. . . ."7 How could the kingdom be within us if the grace of God were not within us? The kingdom of God without the grace of God could not be the kingdom of God because the kingdom of God and the grace of God are synonymous. They are established within us, and they are awaiting our acceptance. We accept them by giving up our will, our desires, our wishes, our hopes, our ambitions, and accepting God's grace, God's will, and God's way. It is the way of peace, holiness, righteousness, harmony, wholeness, completeness, and abundance far beyond our ability to outline.

When we have surrendered all our desires and wishes and begin to receive God, we will wonder how we could have been so niggardly with ourselves as to want only the meager little bit that we have desired in the face of the abundance awaiting us. Who knows what treasures God has laid up for those who love Him? Who knows what treasures God has in store for those who surrender their puny desires, wishes, and will, and let God's grace be fulfilled?

CLEANSING THE TEMPLE

In meditation we clear ourselves of our desires, hopes, longings, and wishes, and establish ourselves in God:

I am satisfied, Father, that Thou art the all-knowing intelligence. I am satisfied that Thou knowest my need before I do. I am more than satisfied that Thy will be done in me and that Thy grace be my sufficiency in all things.

19

In this contemplative meditation, we cleanse the temple of self of our human desires. Then when we are sure that we are empty, the real prayer begins, the prayer in which there are no words and no thoughts. The only attitude of prayer is an empty receptivity: "Thy will be done in me," and then be still and know where God is and what God is.

In the surrender of all desires, we are cleansed and purified; we are a vessel which is empty. We have no words, no thoughts, and for a moment—it could be a second, a minute, it could be five minutes—we are just receptive. We wait, and, whether we know it or not, something takes place. This vacuum that we have created by the emptying of our finite selves is instantaneously filled with the divine Presence. At times we consciously know It and feel It; at other times we do not. It is of no importance, however, whether we know It or whether we feel It. The important thing is that it has happened. There can be no such emptying-out process without a filling-up process, for these are one.

Spirit Fills the Vacuum of Human Self

The moment we have emptied ourselves of self and made room for the Spirit, the Spirit is there. Then we may actually hear these words: "The Spirit of the Lord is upon me, because he hath anointed me to preach the gospel to the poor; he hath sent me to heal the brokenhearted, to preach deliverance to the captives, and recovering of sight to the blind, to set at liberty them that are bruised."[8] These words are spoken from generation to generation, as if they were a perpetual recording going out over the air, but they can be heard only in the silence by those receptive.

When the Spirit of God dwells in us, then do we become the children of God. When does the Spirit of God dwell in us? It has

20

been dwelling within us from everlasting to everlasting, but from the moment of our acknowledgment of It, of our emptiness, and our realization of It, It consciously functions as our life.

Fill me. Let Thy mind be my mind; let Thy life be my life; let Thy Spirit be my spirit.

Let me be empty that Thou mayest enter, and always with the realization that if there be any hidden fault in me I be purified and be willing to surrender.

Then we watch the miracle in transformed lives because we are not now a human being who knows some truth. We are now emptied of being a human being and have become divine by virtue of the Spirit of God which dwells in us.

We cannot influence God to heal anyone, to save anyone, or to perform miracles. But if we surrender our mind, body, soul, and consciousness that it may be filled with the presence of God, God will mold us to Its will, which is the will of good, harmony, health, wholeness, completeness, and perfection.

As we yield ourselves to God, God will make us over in His image and likeness, which is the image and likeness of health, harmony, abundance, and joy. Sometimes we are merely able to prove that manna falls for only one day at a time, that a sufficiency exists day by day where we are for what we need. But in whatever way it comes, it is not going to be your will or my will. It is going to be a yielding to the will of God so that we may be influenced by God.

We must surrender our will to the divine will, and let the presence and power of God do with us as It will. We must surrender, if necessary, even our will to be healthy. We must surrender every personal desire, open ourselves completely, and invite the Father:

21

Fill me; fill me. Let Thy Spirit be present in me. Let It work Its will in me. Let It do with me what It will.

Prayer is not a message from man to God. In its highest sense, prayer is the word of God uttered by God and received by man in his consciousness with signs following. Our praying really is a recognition of the fact that we have wandered into a far country and that we are trying to find our way back home. Therefore, if there is to be any begging or pleading, it is only "Father, awaken me."

· 3 ·

Bringing Our Gift
to the Altar

. . . If thou bring thy gift to the altar, and there rememberest that thy brother hath ought against thee; Leave there thy gift before the altar, and go thy way; first be reconciled to thy brother, and then come and offer thy gift.

—Matthew 5:23, 24

How MANY TIMES have we brought our gift of prayer to God without first making peace with our fellow man! But if we try to pray and still have ought against anyone, still have not forgiven fully, our prayers are wasted. This is one of the reasons prayer is not answered. If we are not at peace or if we are holding anyone in judgment, criticism, condemnation, or ill will, our prayer is of no avail; it does not get through to the throne of God, because it is not possible for prayer to reach God through the mind or consciousness of a person who is not at peace with his fellow man.

If there is anyone who has persecuted us, despitefully used, harmed, or insulted us, there must be a forgiving even unto seventy times seven. We cannot go to the throne of God except pure and humble in Spirit. We can, of course, but it will not do any good as far as prayer is concerned. First, there must be a humility

23

that impels us to make peace with our fellow man. It may well be that we have friends or relatives who will not make peace with us. That is not our problem. It does not mean that we attempt to compel them to be on good terms with us; it means that we, in our hearts, bear no grievance toward anyone.

To pray for someone else's forgiveness has no power, insofar as influencing God in our behalf, but praying for our enemies is a release to us. It is an acknowledgment that we have held somebody in bondage to a wrong and, therefore, it is really asking for our own forgiveness. This act of humility is demanded of us before there can be answered prayer.

Purification Through a Sacrifice of Personal Sense

Some persons waste their opportunity for spiritual salvation because their prayer is for the purpose of bringing something to themselves without a sacrifice of anything within them. A person cannot be the same today as he was yesterday and expect to have his prayers answered. There must be a constant willingness and striving that purification take place, that our sins be taken from us, that our false appetites be removed, and that our selfishness, greed, lust, animosity, resentments, biases, and bigotries be forsaken. There is no way for the Spirit of God to enter in without that inner desire for purification.

Our lives must be lived constantly in the attitude of a willingness to be purified: "I want to be purified. Cleanse me of faults that may be hidden from me." We ourselves do not recognize the depths of our own errors. Even if our friends or relatives tell us about them, we are nearly always quite certain that we do not have them. That is natural. We like to see the better side of our nature.

The point, however, is that in this human scene we do have

24

defects of character that act as barriers to the receptivity to the Spirit of God within us. It is only in the constant desire to be purified through the surrender of self that prayer is answered.

In our work with others, we do not point out their faults and tell them that they must be corrected. Rather do we impersonalize whatever error we notice and realize, "This is not of man. It is the carnal mind, a universal belief, and therefore is not power." In this way our friends, our patients, and our students are freed of their faults, except in those cases where they are so tenaciously determined to hold on to them that they will not relinquish them and will not even recognize that they are there to be surrendered. But on the whole every one of us is more than happy to give up those qualities or traits of character that interfere with his spiritual progress. As we are shown the things about ourselves that require correction, we enter into the spirit of forgiveness.

We cannot attain the realization of God without making of ourselves a fitting temple to receive God. This does not involve first getting healthy or wealthy. It means to understand how to receive God in our consciousness, and the way is to open our ears:

Right now, whether I am in sin, in disease, or in poverty, let me hear the "still small voice."[1] *Let me be receptive when I am riding on the bus or in an automobile; let me be receptive when I am doing housework or marketing; let me always have one area of consciousness in which I am open to that "still small voice."*

This is a preparation for receiving God, but another and most important preparation is living the life of constant forgivingness:

Father, I do not pray that my enemies be destroyed: I pray that they be forgiven. They know not what they do. I pray that Thy grace fill their hearts and Thy forgiveness touch their lives.

Attaining the Attitude and Altitude of Prayer

Prayer which takes an attitude of praying for the world and reaches that high altitude of forgiveness and of praying for the enemy is a way of life. An attitude of forgiveness and the altitude that comes from praying for the enemy must be reached in order that we may be unselfed, because only in being unselfed can the Spirit of God enter in or flow out. Only in that unselfedness does the Spirit of God purify, redeem, and lift up.

It is not that we do not know the human faults of many, nor that we condone the acts of dictators or tyrants, but we must rise high in consciousness before we can really pray, "Father, forgive these tyrants. Forgive those who are causing what may be the destruction of the world. Do not destroy them, Father: forgive them. Open their eyes; open their ears; open their hearts. I do not seek that they be overcome or destroyed. I do not seek revenge, but rather that they be forgiven."

And yet, how many times since the most ancient of days have prayers been for the destruction of the enemy! This alone is a barrier to answered prayer. The moment we pray for the destruction of any enemy, even our nation's enemy, we have cut ourselves off from God.

But I say unto you, Love your enemies, bless them that curse you, do good to them that hate you, and pray for them which despitefully use you, and persecute you;

That ye may be the children of your Father which is in heaven.
—Matthew 5:44, 45

Who is a child of God except one who prays for the enemy, one who forgives seventy times seven? Do we want to be children of God? As children of God, we are heirs of God, joint-heirs to all

26

the heavenly riches. Do we want that? Then the attitude and altitude of prayer demand, not that we spend our entire time praying for our friends and relatives, but that we spend most of our time praying for our enemies. We must put up our sword, our mental sword, and forgive them, for truly they know not what they do.

There is no access to God except through love, and love is not a sensual emotion: love is a state of spiritual integrity, the integrity that enables us to say to ourselves as we go within in prayer:

Here, Father, here I am. In my heart I bear no animosity to any man. Forgive my enemies: the enemies of my nation, the enemies of my race, all those who are enemies of God or man. Let Thy light and Thy grace shine on all mankind. I hold no limitations in my heart; I have no boundaries, no place where I would try to exclude God; but here in my prayer, I open the entire universe to God's grace that all may be equally blessed. The intent of my heart is that the Grace that flows to me will be shared with those who have less.

CARRYING THE CHRIST-PEACE

We are not ready to pray unless we are able to look out at our neighbor and realize, "Christ is as much the center of your being as of my being." We do not condone his faults; we do not agree that he should go on in his evil ways. We understand that all evil is the product of ignorance, and therefore we pray for his forgiveness. When we live in that attitude toward our fellow man, we are in the attitude and the altitude of prayer, and God's grace is flowing through the very flesh and blood of us, flowing into our business and home—but only as we are clear transparencies by holding ourselves in love.

The Master said, " 'My peace I give unto you'[2]—not my judg-

27

ment, my criticism, my condemnation. 'My peace I give unto you: not as the world giveth'—but the spiritual peace, the spiritual Grace—'give I unto you.' "[2] He was the example for us. If we are to live the contemplative or spiritual way of life, our days and nights must be spent in an attitude of "My peace, the spiritual peace of God, I give unto thee." How different that is from praying that we receive God's peace! Imagine what would happen if we could walk the world with that attitude!

Think what wonderful things can happen in our homes when we look upon every member of our family with "My peace I give unto you," instead of "my criticism, my complaint, my judgment." Is it not true that we often reserve our worst conduct for our own home, whereas we should begin with our home and see what miracles come back to us as we live that life of "My peace I give unto you"?

PRAYING WITH AN UNCONDITIONED MIND

We should never permit ourselves to be defiled by thinking defiling thoughts of others. Toward those whom we see in what we think of as sin, our attitude must always be one of forgiveness, not of forgiving them as much as forgiving ourselves for seeing them erroneously. To look out upon the world and its people without prejudice, without bias, without opinion, and without judgment is to pray with an unconditioned mind. It is to realize:

I have no knowledge of you. I do not know if you are young or old, good or bad, sick or well, alive or dead. I know nothing about you. I sit here with an open, unconditioned mind. I will not call you good, and I will not call you bad. I will not call you healthy or unhealthy; I will not call you saint or sinner; I will not call you young or old. Any judgment that I make would be based on appear-

28

ances, and appearances can be deceptive.

I will sit here without a concept, letting the Father within tell me what I need to know about you. Judging by appearances, I have no way of knowing you at all. Therefore, I will listen; I will be instructed.

Then inwardly we are told, "These are *My* beloved children in whom *I** am well pleased. *My* grace is their sufficiency, and someday even the apparently stupid ones will awaken and discover it."

This is what we learn when we look out at the world without judgment, with the unconditioned mind, and let God reveal the truth about the person, situation, or condition. It is true that with a little psychology anyone could tell us a great deal about ourselves humanly, but none of it would be prayer, nor would it be beneficial. One thing alone will benefit us, this truth:

"Know ye not that ye are the temple of God,"[3] *and God dwelleth in you? Thou art the son of God; thou art the child of God. The Spirit of the Lord God dwelleth in you, and you in Him, for ye are one.*

Coming from an unconditioned mind, this is the word of God, "quick, and powerful, and sharper than any two-edged sword."[4] The word of God is the healing, reforming, and redeeming agency. The word of man can flatter us and tell us how good we are, but the word of God goes right through the middle and says, "No, you are not good and you are not bad: you are *Mine.** You are not even you, you are *Me:** you are *My* son, the son of the living God, and the Father and the son are one. Father and son and Holy Spirit are not three but one, and that one is you: Father and son and

*The word *I*, italicized, refers to God.

*The words "Me" and "Mine," capitalized, refer to God.

29

Holy Spirit in you." This, the unconditioned mind reveals.

The conditioned mind says that we are young or old, sick or well, rich or poor; but the unconditioned mind says, " 'Awake thou that sleepest. . . . and Christ shall give thee light.'[5] Awake! Awake, and Christ will give you life, for know now that you are the temple of the living God, the instrument through and as which God lives."

RESPECT FOR THE INDIVIDUAL THROUGH THE REVELATION OF SPIRITUAL IDENTITY

As we rise into the consciousness of this truth and know it, it frees us from the belief that we are human beings in need of forgiveness. It frees us from the belief that we are young or old, sick or well. It reveals to us the truth of the spiritual nature of our being; and that is the only being there is. God is Spirit, and we are the image and likeness of God; therefore, we are spiritual. God is ageless. Thus we are ageless, for we are one with God.

Prayer has many facets, but in the highest prayer we wait for God to give us His word. When He gives us His word, it is the truth about you and about me; it is the truth about God-government on earth. Through this, we will one day witness peace on earth. Then it will not be an interval between wars; it will be a continuous peace. Do not think for a moment that peace can come unless some on earth acknowledge the divinity and Christliness of individual being, unless there are those who acknowledge that Soul, mind, and body are sacred.

In the countries where individuals and individual rights are respected, I have seen the nature of freedom. In some countries I have also seen that no human beings are respected unless they occupy a high place and command a forced respect. I have seen that there is no hope of freedom or justice or equity in those places, and there never will be unless respect comes for one another as individuals. But why are we entitled to respect as individuals? Have you or I done anything to deserve it? God forbid! It is only because we are children of God, because the Spirit of the Lord God dwells in us, that we are entitled to love, honor, and respect from one another and from everyone we contact in the world. If we give that, that is the measure we will receive.

Prayer must be a recognition that God is the Father of all mankind. Prayer that does not include the realization that God's grace is universal and impersonal, that It is for the sinner as well as for the saint at any time the sinner or the saint wishes to open his eyes to It, is not a prayer of spiritual understanding. Prayer, if it includes one, includes the Christ; if it excludes one, excludes the Christ. With an openness of heart that is willing to embrace the entire universe, we become transparencies into which and through which the love of God can flow to the world of men, women, children, friends, and enemies.

This is the attitude of prayer: humility, benevolence, spiritual integrity. There must be no mental reservations. Our heart is open to receive God's grace that It may flow to our neighbor. In this purity of motive, our prayers will be answered.

Breaking the Prison Bars of the Mind

God is omnipresent; God is omniscient, the all-knowing. There is no way to hide from God the intents and the purposes of our hearts, minds, or souls. An absence of answered prayer means that there is need for further purification until we come before the presence of God with a clean heart. "Let the words of my mouth, and the meditation of my heart, be acceptable in thy sight."[6] How can they be, if we have dishonesty in our thought or ill will toward any man? There must be love.

31

The word "love" is heard so much that we may gather the impression that there is a love somewhere that will do something for us. There is not. There is no love in heaven or on earth that will do anything for us except the love that we express. The love that meets our need is the love that flows out through us. It is not the love that comes to us from God; it is not the love that comes to us from other persons, high or low.

The Master taught that love must be expressed in forgiveness, in praying for the enemy, and in all forms of benevolence. When he said, "Verily I say unto you, Inasmuch as ye have done it unto one of the least of these my brethren, ye have done it unto me. . . . Verily I say unto you, Inasmuch as ye did it not to one of the least of these, ye did it not to me,"[7] he was outlining the things that we must do: visit the sick, comfort the comfortless, visit them that are in prison. In prison? Did he mean only those behind prison bars? No, every human being is in prison, imprisoned in his own mind, in his own troubles, in his own problems, in his own false beliefs, in his own hates, animosities, and jealousies.

Is there anywhere in the world a prison equal to that of man's own mind, when that mind is filled with hate, jealousy, envy, lust, malice, resentment, or antagonism? Is there any prison greater than the prison of fear? So we must visit our friends and our enemies in their particular prisons and release them. And we can! We can release all who come to us from their prisons, but only in one way: by releasing that divine love that holds no one in bondage. If we look out upon men and women and see them good or bad, young or old, sick or well, we are malpracticing them, and they feel themselves in some kind of bondage. They feel the prison of sin, disease, or age that we have placed them in mentally. We set them free, however, if we can realize:

Every sense of mortal error is an impersonal activity, an impersonal or universal belief, and is no part of you whatsoever. You, yourself, are the kingdom of God; you are actually the temple of God, and God is in the temple which you are.

You have only one Father: God, Spirit. You have no human heritage whatsoever because the whole story of your human birth is a lie. God is your Father. Spirit is the creative principle of your being. Spirit is the essence and substance of your mind, your Soul, your being, and even your body is the temple of the living God.

In that awareness, we remove the prison bars of belief from every person. We loose him from a universal mental malpractice, from the belief that he is a mortal, born in sin and created to die. Our prayers will not be answered until we can look out at all the world and realize:

Father, forgive me that I have misjudged Your creation, that I have ever offended any of Your creation, that I have sat in judgment upon them, withheld forgiveness from them, hated, envied, or malpracticed them in any way.

Father, forgive me for seeing out of mortal eyes, not out of Your eyes. I was "blind" with mortal sight, but now I see. Now I see that there is but one Father, and we of this earth are of that spiritual household, all members of one spiritual family.

Whenever the spirit of love is entertained within us, freedom comes from whatever our particular prison may be. All the negative qualities of human thought are prisons, and every one of us wants to be loosed from these prisons. None of us really wants to hate any more than we want to be hated. None of us wants to be feared any more than we want to fear. None of us wants to be in disease any more than we want to see anyone else in disease. The

33

only way to break our fetters is to break the fetters of those who enter our spiritual household, our consciousness.

THROUGH FORGIVENESS, WE REACH THE ALTAR

In the degree that we permit love to flow out from us, some who are receptive and responsive will be healed: physically, mentally, morally, financially, or in whatever way their need may be. If, however, there were not a receptive person in all the world to be blessed by our love and truth, we ourselves would be blessed.

It is impossible for us to come to the throne of God pure of spirit and not draw unto us all those ready to be forgiven, all those ready to be healed or to be enriched. "I, if I be lifted up from the earth, will draw all men unto me"[8]—not all who exist in the world, but all who are ready, receptive, and responsive. We could sit in our home alone with no one knowing what is taking place in our consciousness, and by the next day some persons would ask for our prayers, for help, for healing, and we might wonder how they knew. There is only one Soul, one Spirit, one Consciousness. Whatever is in my consciousness that is pure draws unto me those who have need of that.

In loving mankind we are loving the Christ, and only in the love that we express to mankind are we expressing love to the Christ. The prayer that brings the demonstration of God's grace into the fullness of our lives is the prayer in which we go to God with a pure heart.

I am not asking for Your power over anything or anybody. I do not want You to destroy my enemies. I ask You to forgive my enemies.

Father, search my heart, cleanse it, remove whatever is in it of

34

an erroneous nature, and let Your grace descend upon me. You
know the intents of my heart. May Your grace be upon me.

With that attitude, it will not be long before we have developed
enough of the fourth-dimensional consciousness so that we will
receive answers.

Prayer itself will come to us in that moment when our consciousness is purified and we stand in the presence of God, completely still, without any desire except one:

Here I am. Fill me! Be my mind; be my soul; be my spirit.

I seek nothing of Thee, God. I seek only to be an instrument
through which Thy grace, Thy love, Thy forgiveness, Thy supply,
and Thy infinite presence flow through me and out into the world.

In this there is no earthly or material desire. When we have
purified and prepared ourselves, prayer becomes an attitude of
listening. The ear is open, and into it flows that Spirit of God—
but only if we have purified ourselves, only if we are now praying
for the enemy, only if we are forgiving seventy times seven, only
if we are sharing our little cruse of oil or cake of meal. From now
on we are not receivers: we are transparencies through which the
grace of God flows. Whereas before we may have been the man
of earth, seeking something, now we are the children of God
through whom God's blessings flow to those yet in darkness.

Through prayer we make contact with the Spirit within and
thus we commune with our Source and bring forth spiritual fruitage. We look out upon the world with no animosity, no remembrance of grievances, with full forgiveness of those who have
offended us personally, racially, or nationally. At this moment, we
are not sitting in judgment on anyone, nor holding him in criticism or condemnation. If we cannot at the moment feel forgive-

35

ness, at least we can ask the Father within to do the forgiving for us and pray that the enemy be awakened, forgiven, illumined, and enlightened.

That we ourselves have been guilty of offenses of omission and of commission, no one knows better than we do. We also know that no greater gift could come to us than to know this moment that we are forgiven: forgiven by God and forgiven by man, with our slate wiped clean. What greater gift can there be than to know that no one anywhere on earth, nor anyone who has ever gone beyond this earth, is holding us in judgment, in unforgiveness, in hate, or in animosity! This same boon is expected of us: to forgive as we would be forgiven.

In this act of cleansing ourselves, remember that we are opening our consciousness to the inflow of the Spirit, to the cleansing of our mind and body, and thereby to harmony, to health, and to peace because we are now at peace with all mankind.

We robe ourselves in the royal robes of the Spirit; we place upon our finger the jewel of spiritual authority, so that we may say, "Neither do I condemn or judge thee. Thy sins be forgiven thee. God's grace be thy sufficiency." We say it with the God-given authority of children of God, heirs of God, royal princes of the household of God, bold enough eventually to say, "I and the Father are one. 'He that seeth me seeth him that sent me.'9 All that the Father has is mine to share with you."

· 4 ·

This Is Immortality

LIFE, REAL LIFE, is lived in consciousness; it is lived in the secret place within ourselves. We do not begin to suspect what the God-life can be until we have contacted that fountain of Life within us. We are not really living if we think of life as something that exists between what is called birth and death. This is not life.

This life is, as one of the ancient mystics called it, a parenthesis in eternity. It is often pictured as a circle and is usually spoken of as being eternal. But if we live only inside the parenthesis that begins with birth and ends at death, we are missing the greatest part of life, the eternal, infinite, and immortal structure in which we discover God's creation. In this brief interval called the parenthesis, we live largely in man's creation, and we miss God's creation. We miss the life and love of God; we miss sharing in the life and love of one another.

If we know each other only as human beings, we are cheating ourselves of a tremendous delight. We are offspring of God, filled with the love, the life, and the Spirit of God, and this we must recognize. All the joys of spiritual being are embodied in us for sharing. That is why we are on earth.

When the Master said, "I am come that they might have life, and that they might have it more abundantly,"[1] did he mean that

37

one man out of all the world's history had come to earth that we might have life? No, he meant that *I* within each one of us has come that you and I might enjoy a more abundant life with each other. He also said that he had come to bring resurrection and life eternal. Then why have you and I come? Would it not be a sad commentary on God, if one of us were here to bring joy, peace, health, and freedom to the world, and the rest of the world were to do nothing but sit back and receive it?

It would be unfortunate if it were given only to a dozen mystics to know and enjoy God and the spiritual nature of mankind. But life is not like that at all. It appears to be only because we have circumscribed life by giving our attention to the baubles of life: to our work, our profession, our home, our family. Some of us may think we were born for such purposes, but these were meant only to be facets to take up part of our time, while we are discovering the true meaning of life, of eternality and immortality.

We were given the grace of God to share with one another. This is a universal truth and a universal relationship that everyone has with God. We will not discover it, however, in life out in the world. We will discover it in the life that we lead within our own being as we learn through prayer and meditation to be taught of God and to receive impartations of spiritual wisdom.

The human life we live is nothing but a dream. We are here for a span of a few years and then are gone. That is not the purpose of life. If that were all there is to life, we should not grieve at all when our friends and relatives pass on or die. They are not missing anything by leaving here because many of them did not have too much while they were here.

If we did not know the full truth, we could grieve when in our brief lifetime we see so many of the youth of our country killed, wounded, and rendered mentally infirm. To see such a waste of life could cause us grief but for one thing. We have glimpsed reality; we have glimpsed immortality; and we know that in spite of the mistakes that have been made that caused their death and destruction, they will have another chance to live and to fulfill themselves.

LEARNING TO PRAY THAT THE PURPOSE OF LIFE AS FULFILLMENT MAY BE REVEALED

We could avoid all the inharmonies and discords of human experience if we knew how to pray, if we knew the function and method of prayer, because prayer is our contact with the infinite Source that maintains the harmony, the peace, the wholeness, and the completeness of mankind. We cannot, by might or by power, make our life beautiful, but we can fulfill our nature through an understanding of the function of prayer and its practice.

God created you and me spiritually in His image and likeness, imbued us with His life, His nature, His character, His qualities, and His quantities, and because of that this great capacity for fulfillment exists within every single one of us. The purpose of life on earth is to bring forth that capacity, to bring forth that beauty, harmony, and grace in lives of joy and fulfillment. That is the original purpose of the life of spiritual man as it was meant to be lived in the Garden of Eden, that is, in divine harmony.

We lost this capacity because we lost the ability to turn within, to open out a way to let beauty, harmony, and grace be expressed. We began to search in the outer realm for the Holy Grail. We traveled all the way around the world, and for what? Contentment, peace, joy, harmony, rest! Were we successful in our search? Of course not, because we had to take ourselves around the world as we traveled, and the self that we took around the world is the self that had not found its home in God. But when the self finds its home in God, it can travel or remain at home and find eternal

39

bliss and eternal opportunities for service, for dedication to God and to man, in an exchange of good.

With the practice of prayer, a measure of harmony begins to be restored in our daily life. Some of the first fruits of prayer are health, a greater sense of abundance, or happier human relationships. These are not the end and aim of prayer. The end and aim of prayer is that we discover our eternal life, the life that was lived before birth, the life that will be lived after the grave, so that we can encompass right here on earth the totality of spiritual existence, a divine and ageless existence.

Is it not foolish to relegate all the pleasures of life to children, all the cares of life to adults, and all the woes of life to the aged? This is not really living, is it? Living begins when we are able to perceive the nature of our real life, the life that we began living in the beginning when we existed in the bosom of our Father, the life that we live when we know ourselves as we really are.

The Master revealed that his kingdom was not of this world. Yet many of us spend most of our time worrying about this world, as if what is taking place from day to day were the most important part of our existence. I do not mean that we should neglect this life on earth, but that we should spiritualize it—not make it a matter of just living in the flesh, living for the dollars, or living in the comforts, but actually living in and through the Soul, so that we live in and through the beauty that God created.

The real beauty is the Presence that formed this world, the Spirit that animates it, the divine Grace that takes a barren tree and in a short time fills it with leaves and blossoms and fruit. To know this Grace is far greater than to enjoy the flowers after they are on the bushes or to eat the fruit from the tree. To be able to know the Spirit that produces these, to live with this Spirit and watch It function in our experience, watch It bring forth fruitage in our lives, this is the supreme joy.

Many persons, after discovering the nature of prayer and meditation, leave the world in order to live wholly in that Withinness. To me, of course, it seems that they miss something. In my meditations and my periods of aloneness, I see the forces that operate behind the world that make you and me what we are, that make nature what it is, but then I like to go outside, too, and enjoy the fruitage of it out there.

The life of prayer and meditation brings into our outer lives a far greater capacity to live than we ever knew before because now we are not living with that part of us which is a part of mortality. We are now living with the whole of us, the Spirit, the Soul, and the Consciousness, and therein lies the joy.

DISCOVERING THE INVISIBLE SOUL OF ONE ANOTHER AND OF THE UNIVERSE

Most of you can know me only as a suit of clothes and a white shirt, but that is not what I am at all. I really have a life, not a life that began with birth and ends in the grave. That is not my life at all. That is just how I happen to spend a few decades in the totality of life. But I have a life that is anchored in eternity, that began long before my birth and will blossom out more after the passing than in the years preceding that passing. It is a life of joy that is not dependent on how many dollars I have in my pocket because that joy was there when there were no dollars in the pocket, and it would be there if there were no dollars now. It is a joy that has its source, not only in knowing myself, but in knowing you.

There is a *you* that I have met within myself; there is a *you* that I love to be with; there is a *you* that I have traveled all over the world to meet. This is the *you* that God made in His own image and likeness, and it is a *you* that existed before you were born. It

41

is a *you* that I not only know, but that I will continue to know when you are no longer on the face of the globe because I do not lose sight of you if you or I should decide to leave this phase of life.

"Before Abraham was, I am."[2] This is true of me; this is true of you. You must have some interest in knowing yourself as you have existed in God and as you will continue to exist in God throughout all time. It must interest you to know your parents and your children, not as they look in their physical frames, but what the Soul of them reveals, what God placed in them and what, for the most part, has been kept hidden throughout their span on earth.

While I could read in books that you are spiritual and that you are the child of God, this would never make me know it, nor would it ever make me acquainted with you. It would only give me some information about you which I might or might not believe and which I certainly would not believe if I judged by appearances. However, having been lifted up to that point where my heavenly Father could impart truth, I then behold you as you are, because I first beheld myself. I saw myself in the image and likeness of God; I saw myself as spiritual being existing before my birth and still living after my death. Because I saw that, I saw your identity. It was only then that I began to love people, to want to be with them, to travel to meet them, and to learn about them and from them, and share with them.

Divine love, spiritual love, and understanding can come into our hearts only when we have been lifted up so high that we discern the real nature of one another. Until then, all we see are the human limitations each one has. In that moment when in prayer and meditation we behold the nature of Christ, the spiritual man, then we begin a life on earth of spiritual love, spiritual sharing, and spiritual grace.

REINCARNATION

God expresses Itself as individual Life from everlasting to everlasting. It never incarnates; It can never reincarnate. From the standpoint of God as Life, there could be no reincarnation because there is no incarnation. There is just a state of divine Being. Our body, the form that we use here, is but a cover for, or a hiding of, the life that we really are.

In our human sense, we have incarnated and we will reincarnate. It appears that we are a life within a Life. It is as if there were two of us: the one who sits here writing, and the real One, which is the intelligence, the life, and the being of my individual Self. *I*, in my true identity, have never been born, *I* will never die, and *I* cannot be reborn. That part of me which is visible as Joel was born into the belief of two powers, will pass out of it, and will reincarnate, unless during this lifetime I come into the realization of my true identity. Then I will not have to reincarnate.

That make-believe life of Joel will keep on making believe over and over again, until there is a "dying daily" leading to the final death of personal sense. What we behold with our eyes is but a form. The form changes, but the life does not change.

If we judge by appearances, we might think that you and I are gradually dying because each day some part of this form is dying and being reborn again. But am *I* dying every day and being reborn? No, *I* am intact, *I* am complete. Someday each one of you will have to realize what I am saying to you: I am *I*. I am that *I AM*, I always have been, and I always will be. Should the time come when, instead of just sloughing off a little of this form each day, the whole thing drops away, I will still be *I*. In that awareness, there will be no need for me to reincarnate, because I will have already died to the belief that this form is "me." This body is only

43

the instrument that I have been walking around with and using. It is the vehicle, the visible form, but I, myself, am not in it.

So it is that what you see in the mirror is not you. You are the one who is seeing, but you are not that which is seen because you are looking out from behind your eyes and are beholding not you but your body.

Travel up and down your body, and you will become convinced that the body is not you. There is a *you* that possesses this body, but can you find that *you* anywhere inside the body? Search as you will, you are not in your body, and you are not your body. Then, who are you? You are *I,* and your body is an instrument like the form of a tree—the bark, the root, the leaves—an instrument showing forth the glory of the invisible tree. And so are you. You are the showing forth of the glory of the invisible *I,* that *I* that is one with God.

Preparing for the Experience of Immortality

When you see a leaf dying or withering on a tree or fruit dropping from a tree, remember that it is not the life that is dying: it is the form that is changing. The leaf, the orange, the peach, the apple—these are forms, but the life remains to produce more leaves next year, more blossoms, more fruit.

You are life: you are not body. In the moment that you recognize that you are life, living through the body, you are prepared for the experience of immortality because then you will know that, even when the day comes that this body drops away, you will be there forming another body, just as the life of the tree is still there ready to form the leaves, the blossoms, and the fruit of the new season. Eventually you can see that the *I* of you keeps on forming more and better bodies, more and more mature bodies unto eternity.

44

Since "I and my Father are one,"[3] *I will coexist with God eternally. I will live forever in the bosom of the Father, for I and my Father are inseparable and indivisible. Neither life nor death will ever separate me from the life and the love of God, for I am life. I am truth, I am Spirit, I am incorporeal, I am eternal. I will never pass away. Forms—yes; but not I. I will be here forever.*

Until you realize this, you cannot fully benefit from the teaching of Jesus, which is that the life of God is your life. This constitutes your immortality.

Dying does not ensure immortality. Immortality is an activity of truth in your consciousness and can just as well be experienced while you are on earth as in any future lifetime. In order to experience immortality, however, you must understand the nature of your own being. Unless you know what you are you cannot experience immortality. Immortality is an experience which you may have here and now if within yourself you can realize *I:*

The I *that I am is of the same spiritual substance as God; the* I *that I am is of the same truth-substance as God; the* I *that I am is of the same love-substance as God. Therefore the* I *that I am is incorporeal, spiritual, pure, infinite, and It has given me this body to live It.*

The I *that I am has brought this body from infancy to maturity, and It will keep right on until this body falls away and* I *immediately appear in my new form. Just as the life of the tree appears in that new form of the seed, so the life of the seed appears in the new form of the tree. The life of the tree appears in the new form of the new leaves, the new buds, and the new blossoms, and yet it is always that same life, always that indivisible life which is God.*

That life which I *am is always in the bosom of the Father, never separate and apart from the infinite divine Life, therefore, omni-*

present. I am always present, and the Master, who is Omnipresence, is always present where I am, and all the masters of all the ages, all the masters of all the religions, all the masters of all the great mystical teachings. The life of all of us is united because of Omnipresence, and when I am in meditation I become consciously aware of the truth that I and the Father are one, and in that oneness I am present with the saints and the sages of all times. Wherever the consciousness of God is, there are the saints, sages, and revelators, all embodied in God-consciousness.

When you turn within to the God-consciousness of your being, always remember that you are uniting with everyone of spiritual light. Every person who has received the Spirit of God is right there where you are in God-consciousness, and all are making their contributions to you. Omnipresence is what they have demonstrated, and Omnipresence is what we are seeking to demonstrate. Unless you can sing that word morning, noon, and night and know that you are declaring the omnipresence of the Spirit of God within you, the omnipresence of the divine Life, you are not really coming into the experience of your immortality.

While you are out busying yourself with the things of the world, you have no time or opportunity to receive God's revelation of Himself, the revelation of Truth Itself within you. So learn to set aside time for an inner communion with the Spirit of God that is always within you that It may reveal Itself to you and give you Its grace, Its truth, Its healing and freeing influence.

Thy presence is within me functioning to set me free from the limitations of sense and mortal belief, to set me free in my spiritual identity.

Do not wait for immortality to come at some later time. If you are not experiencing it, retire into a meditation in which you

46

realize the omnipresence of the life of God as your life. If you do not succeed today or tonight, go peacefully and quietly to sleep, but remember that tomorrow you owe yourself a debt, and that is to return again in meditation to the realization of the omnipresence of the life of God as your life. Continue doing this whether it takes a day, a week, a month, or a year. Continue until the "still small voice"[4] says to you, "I will never leave you nor forsake you, for I am come that you might have life eternal." Then you will be living your immortality.

It will really make no difference to you then whether you live on this plane or on another, nor will you be so deeply grieved as your friends depart from this plane. You will realize they have merely dropped one particular form of life in order to appear as another.

The reason we do not grieve when a child is born is that we are hiding from ourselves the fact that with every birth there will also come a passing, but because that passing is somewhere off in the future, we refuse to be concerned about it. So we rejoice at birth. It is only some years later that we anticipate that passing and then begin to have the regrets that we might as well have had at the birth. It was just as inevitable then as it is now, and there should be no regrets.

One of the first essentials on this Path is to lose the fear of death. There is but one way to lose that fear or dread, and that is to accept Paul's statement, "Neither death, nor life . . . shall be able to separate us from the love of God."[5] Once you have accepted that, you no longer have any fear or dread of death because you are just as secure in God's love in death as in life.

We do not deny the fact that eventually there is a transition from the human plane. Why not begin to understand it instead of fearing it and hating it, and recognize it as merely a change of locale, a change from one state or form of life to another, but

THE ALTITUDE OF PRAYER

always under the government of God? Neither life nor death can separate us from the government of God, from the love, the care, and the life of God. Once we have that awareness, death has no sting, and when the sting is gone out of death, death itself becomes impossible.

There is no way to prevent death except to lose the fear and dread of it and to understand that in what the world calls life or death, there is a oneness with God, with love, and with life. If you really accept that, you cannot believe that a time will ever come when that relationship with God will change. Therefore, in the experience of life, the experience of death, the experience before our birth, or the experience after our death, we still are one with our Source.

This, too, is prayer. This, too, is contemplation. It is just as legitimate to contemplate death as to contemplate life because in the eyes of God, life and death are one; light and dark are one; here and there are one; youth and old age are one. In the eyes of God, we are all one in our spiritual identity; but remember, it is only the life of contemplation that enables us to meet God within our own consciousness and to live the spiritual life, showing forth the fruitage in happier relationships, in greater abundance of tangible supply, and in a greater degree of health. Thus, the within becomes the without. The degree of our conscious oneness with God within becomes the degree of manifested harmony in the without.

THROUGH SPIRITUAL DISCERNMENT, IMMORTALITY IS REVEALED

We are living an immortal life. It is not we who are really living our life; it is God who is living it. "I live; yet not I, but Christ liveth in me,"[6] and the Christ is immortal and eternal. The life of the

48

Christ is forever. The life of the Christ is embodied in you and in me. It is your very life; It is my very life. It will never leave us. It will go with us from glory to glory, from manifestation to manifestation. We appear today as a baby and tomorrow as an adult, and again as a baby and again as an adult, but it is always *I* who am appearing, always the life of the Christ that is appearing as individual you and me.

Only in meditation is this revealed, and it is in these periods of meditation that the innermost secrets of the spiritual kingdom are revealed to us. Through meditation, spiritual discernment is developed, and through spiritual discernment it is possible for the kingdom of God to reveal itself to you from within you. Without the capacity for spiritual discernment, be assured that the Kingdom cannot reveal itself to you. Although you may find books or Scriptures which tell of that Kingdom, even then you will not grasp what is being revealed to you, because it is really the Spirit of God that bears witness with your individual spirit and reveals to you through spiritual means the secrets of the Kingdom.

Someday you will have an experience and learn that you are *I*, that your Self cannot be confined in time or in space, but that you exist beyond time and beyond space. Then you will know the secret of preexistence. You will know that "before Abraham was, I am," and *I* will be with you unto the end of the world, whether *I*, Joel, say that, or whether *I*, you, say it, for there is only one *I* on this earth. That *I* is the identity of those who have gone out of our physical sight; It is our identity; and It is the identity of those still unborn.

And that is immortality.

49

· 5 ·

God Is Omnipotent

IF WE EVER HOPE to reach the height of prayer, a further preparatory step must be taken, without which there is no way to receive
God or to remove the barrier that has heretofore separated us from
the kingdom of God. That step is to know that God is the only
power and that there is no more power in mind or thought than
there is in matter, and we must know why. We can use the mind
for good or we can use the mind for evil—it all depends upon our
nature. We can use our thoughts to heal or to malpractice. We
can use the power of mind to give a person his freedom or to
dominate him and hold him in slavery.

Look around the world and see if there are not some persons
being held in religious ignorance and supersitition. And are not
whole nations being held in slavery through the mental power of
false ideologies? Does not the advertising world in many cases use
the power of mind and thought falsely and ignorantly to catch our
unwary dollars? When we begin to see these things, then we can
understand that mind and thought with their good and evil are not
of God. Because they are not of God, they are not power. Only
God, Spirit, is power, and besides Spirit there is no other power.

All of us have probably given treatments and watched colds, flu, and dozens of other things dissolve just by knowing that there are no material powers. Now go further and release people from cancer, tuberculosis, and polio by knowing that the son of God is not held in any mental bondage, and that there is no supersititon, fear, or ignorance to hold him in slavery. This universe is governed by law; Spirit is the only lawgiver; and the only law with real power is spiritual law.

Thank You, Father, that You are Spirit and that Spirit is the only power. There are no powers on earth for You to destroy, for You to overcome, for You to remove. Your law alone is power, and Your law is a spiritual law governing all creation. I am not turning to You to destroy evil: I am turning to You in gratitude that I have learned that evil is not power, not material evil or mental evil. I am turning within in peace, because now I have nothing to fear.

All fear departs from us in this truth: God has no pleasure in our dying. He has not provided any disease to take us away, nor has He provided any accidents to kill us. He has provided nothing to call us home to His bosom. Such a belief is a kind of mental slavery that would try to make us believe that God is the author of life and of death, the author of spiritual law and also of a destructive material or mental law. There is no material or mental law in the presence of God, for God alone is law, and the kingdom of God's law is within.

Thank You, Father; I can pray in peace because I am not praying to have You do anything. I am praying the prayer of gratitude and recognition of Your presence. "Where the Spirit of the Lord is, there is liberty"[1]; there is freedom from sin, disease, lack, and limitation, not because You are a power over some other powers, but because You are light, and where light is, darkness cannot exist.

51

Light does not remove darkness. Its presence proves that there is no darkness. The darkness does not go anywhere. In the light of spiritual discernment, disease does not go anywhere. The light reveals the absence of sin, disease, age, lack, limitation, hate, jealousy, and animosity.

INSTEAD OF TAKING THOUGHT, BECOME RECEPTIVE TO GOD

Do you not see that if thought can be loving and hateful, if it can be pure and sinful, it cannot be of God, nor can it be empowered of God? When you know this, the only thought that can have power in your experience is the thought that is imparted to you from the Spirit within. It is neither good nor evil: it is spiritual. It is neither good nor evil: it is harmonious. It is neither good nor evil: it is eternal, immortal, and infinite.

In prayer and meditation, we do not think thoughts of evil or thoughts of good. We *receive* thoughts from God, and when we hear the "still small voice,"[2] the earth of error is shattered; it melts. "Which of you by taking thought can add one cubit unto his stature?"[3] Thought is not power: thought will not make a white hair black; thought will not turn disease into health; thought will not turn health into disease. But the Spirit of God in us reveals divine harmony where sin, disease, death, lack, and limitation appear to the human senses.

Abide in Me *and let* Me *abide in you. Abide in* My *word of truth and let* My *word of truth abide in you, and* I *will make your way healthy, harmonious, peaceful, and joyous.*

Do not trust to the good powers of matter or fear the bad powers of matter; do not trust to the good thoughts of men or fear the bad thoughts of men, for none of these is power. I *in the midst of you*

52

am mighty; I in the midst of you am the Almighty. I in the midst of you am Omnipotence.

When you can close your eyes and know no fear, and not seek for God to do something, see what happens as you settle down into an inner peace:

Thank You, Father; I can abide in peace, for there is no other power. There are no powers to fear; there are no powers for You to do something about. You alone are power; You alone are presence. Your kingdom is established in me; Your grace is my sufficiency in all things. No longer do I seek You as a power; no longer do I accept the power of matter or of mind. Now I accept You and You alone in me.

I have no problems for You to work on, God. I have no powers for You to overcome or destroy. I have come here to commune, to receive Your grace, to receive Your light.

Prayer has sometimes been a frustrating experience because we have turned to God as if God were some great power over evil powers, and as if we were going to ask God to take out His whip and get after the particular devil that is bothering us. The devil may be sin, false appetite, disease, sometimes a person, and we try to get God to do something about it for us. What a waste of time this has been for the thousands of years it has been practiced!

Christ Jesus taught us above all other things not to entreat God to be a power because God already is omnipotence. There is no other power. There is no place in the four Gospels where Jesus ever asked God to do anything for the people, not even to multiply loaves and fishes. His answer to every form of disease was, " 'Arise, take up thy bed, and go unto thine house.'[4] What hinders you from seeing? Open your eyes!"

53

To find the secret of answered prayer, we begin, as did Jesus, with an absolute conviction that God is, and because we have this conviction, we know that God must be omnipotence, the all-power. If God is the all-power, there is nothing to fear from the power of sin, disease, lack, or the power of bullets. Once we begin to perceive the nature of God, to catch the slightest glimpse of God as Omnipotence, and refuse to ask God to destroy any enemy for us, we begin to experience answers to our prayers.

No Resistance to Evil

"Resist not evil."[5] Resist not because God is the all-power and evil is not a power. When we rest in His word, we discover what the enemy does to itself and watch the invisible Power come forth to be our salvation. Have we ever given the invisible Power a chance to save us? Have we not always been too ready to save ourselves? Have we not always had a material or a mental remedy, a material protection or offense, and so have never taken advantage of the opportunity to rest in the Word?

Those of us who are in the spiritual healing ministry must rely on the principle of "put up again thy sword,"[6] that is, do not look for a God-power—just rest in the Word. This condition has only temporary power. The practitioner of spiritual healing who abides in that truth does not resort to material or mental means. He abides in the Word: God is the only power.

The principles of prayer must be known and practiced until it becomes natural for us to say to evil of any name or nature:

You—sin, disease, false appetite, lack, limitation, wars and rumors of wars—could have no power over me, for God alone is power unto me. You could have no power over me because you have no power. God is the substance of this universe. God is the only law of this universe.

Then we must stand until we have proved it. We do not prove it merely because we know these words. Only in the practice of it do we develop the consciousness that makes this true.

THE IMPERSONAL POWER GENERATED THROUGH STILLNESS

Once we know the nature of God and prayer, we come to the place where, by being still, a power is generated in us which is not of ourselves. The power is of God and is brought forth into active manifestation by our ability to be still. "Be still, and know that I am God,"[7] and then rest in that Word.

Spiritual power never operates for your good or my good; it cannot be used; it cannot be channeled or directed. There is no way of praying for your particular good or mine because in the eyes of God there is no "you" or "me" separate from all the other children of God. There would be no way to gain God's grace for you or for me or to direct God's presence or power to this individual or that individual. This is a personalized concept of Deity that has wrecked the religions of the world and has made prayer as ordinarily practiced ineffectual.

Only when God is understood to be a presence and power universally and equally available to all, only in that consciousness in which we do not see each other as separate and apart from the divine Being, can spiritual power flow. If we were to sit quietly, recognizing the invisible presence and power of God permeating all being, anyone who is receptive and in tune with divine love would receive blessings and benediction, Grace in some form or other. It might be as comfort, as peace, as greater health, or as some form of greater abundance, but it would happen; whereas, if an individual were to try to direct God's grace to someone, he would be outside the realm of spiritual power, and he would fail.

THE POWER OF GOD USES US IN A MOMENT OF RECEPTIVITY

It is true that on the mental level of life there are ways of benefiting one another by the power of suggestion and by the power of faith. This has to do with mental power, which can be directed for good or evil or for the benefit or harm of an individual. A power that can be used either for good or evil is not God-power: it is mental power. The power of God cannot be used: the power of God uses us.

Spiritual power functions only when we make ourselves a complete receptivity to the Spirit of God, realizing ourselves as transparencies through which God can function. Then we must have enough humility to know that we cannot tell God what God does not already know. It is the highest form of egotism to try to inform or influence God.

Humility recognizes that the only master there is on earth is a servant. All those who seek to become masters fail. So few are seeking to become servants, and it is the servant whom others eventually call "Master." This is true of everyone who at some time or other has been named a master. They are not only servants of God, but servants of those they come to serve on earth. The master is always working twenty hours a day while the disciple is sleeping his eight hours and enjoying holidays. The master is always serving often even the least of these. Few become masters because few understand that mastership consists of servanthood. Only those who can empty themselves and become transparencies for the action of the Invisible, without attempting to direct, influence, or inform It, can hope to reach some degree of mastery of the subject of spiritual living.

Enter into your sanctuary; shut the door of the senses; and there, in receptivity, await the annunciation, the birth of the Christ, the hearing of the "still small voice." God is not in the storm; God is not in the whirlwind; God is not in words or thoughts. God is in the silence that is heard only when there is an absence of words and thoughts and a receptivity to the inner Presence and Power. Then, and then only, is spiritual power being made manifest on earth. There must be the moment when "ye think not."[8] You must come to an inner conviction that you are never going to be able to demonstrate spiritual power except in the degree that you receive impartations from within. Once you are receiving inner impartations, the power of Spirit operating through you is no longer limited just to you or to the persons around you.

Anyone, from any circle or station in life, whether it be a carpenter, a housewife, or the head of state, can become a voice to the world and a power because it is not the person who becomes that at all. It is the Spirit that is imparting Itself to the individual, and it is the same Spirit that functioned in Krishna and Buddha, Moses and Elijah, that functioned in Jesus, John, and Paul, the same Spirit appearing in these many forms in many lands.

As It appears on earth today, It is still that same Spirit. That is why It knows no limitation. It can take a housewife and make her name internationally famous. It can take a person from any walk of life and make him known throughout the world, not by virtue of what the individual is or does, but by virtue of his receptivity to this infinite Being, infinite Presence, infinite Power.

The Ultimate: Realization of One Selfhood

This is the beginning of a new era, a preparatory stage, which may be called the age of love-thy-neighbor-as-thyself. This will be followed by the final revelation which comes with an understanding of the nature of spiritual power.

Spiritual power has never been known except to the mystics and to their immediate followers. Even where the secret of spiritual power was revealed, it was quickly lost within the second or third generation after the passing of the leader who revealed it. But in this age, spiritual power has been revealed in such a way that it will never be lost. It will spread until it embraces all human consciousness, or rather until all human consciousness embraces it. Then we will be living in the stage which is to come after the period of love-thy-neighbor-as-thyself, when there will no longer be a neighbor or a personal self: there will be only the conscious, realized one Self, that Self which I am, that Self which you are, besides which there is no other.

Then it will be recognized that I am thou, and thou art I, and that there is but one Selfhood. Whatever it is that is to bless me must bless you. Whatever it is that blesses you must bless me, because there is not a "me" and a "thee." There is only the one divine spiritual Being, infinitely manifested as your being and as mine. This One is the life of the universe, the life of you and the life of me. It is the mind and the intelligence of the universe, the mind of you and the mind of me. There is but one Father, one Life, one Principle, one Soul, and It is common to all of us. We do not share parts of It, but the fullness of It appears as individual being, individual you and individual me.

SPIRITUAL POWER IS REVEALED THROUGH PRAYER

How is the nature of spiritual power to be revealed? The answer is in one word: prayer. Only those who have been mystically taught know the meaning of real prayer through which spiritual power is

58

revealed and spiritual harmony is brought into the experience of man on earth.

Our good does not come by might or by power. It cannot come by wars or by human agreements; it cannot come by any form of power that has ever been discovered. Harmony on earth and good will among men cannot be manufactured. There is no human plan broad enough to encompass it or to bring it about because in the human picture some measure of self-interest must always appear, and this self-interest is the only devil there is, individually or collectively.

Only when self-interest is ruled out can spiritual power come in; and self-interest cannot be ruled out while there is a "you" and a "me," separate from each other. As long as there is a possibility of one usurping something of another, one gaining something from another, one losing something to another, self-interest must predominate. When my interest becomes your interest and your interest becomes mine, when we realize that in the progress and prosperity of each other lie the progress and the prosperity of all, only then can we rule out personal sense, personal interest, and make room for the activity of spiritual power in our midst.

The great barrier to God is the belief that there are material and mental powers. Once this belief has been overcome, you are a free individual inside yourself, ready to receive instruction in living and in loving. Then, and then alone, you will learn how to love your neighbor as yourself because you are done with problems. Now you are done with seeking God, seeking happiness, and seeking prosperity. Do not seek any of these. They are the added things. But you never will find this inner peace while you believe in the power of God and other powers besides God.

In Thy presence is fulfillment. Release me now from the belief in powers, for there are no powers on earth except the God-power that creates, maintains, and sustains this universe.

This preparation for prayer, then, is the step in which we surrender the belief in two powers, and settle ourselves back in the comfort of the truth that there is no power to be used, that *I* alone am power, and we *let* the power of God use us.

· 6 ·

Pray Without Ceasing

EVERY HUMAN BEING is born under the law, not under Grace, but under the law of matter, the law of mind, the law of human happenstance, the law of accident, chance, and change.

Parents do not know what kind of a child they may bring forth, and no one can guarantee that any newborn child will be perfect. No parents, regardless of how much love they give their child, can be certain that he will reach manhood or that he will be a person of morals and integrity. Why? Because in their hearts they believe that everything depends on chance, luck, circumstances, or conditions. Who knows when an accident will take place? Who knows when a bomb will be dropped, a call come to go to war; and death, accident, or insanity follow? Who knows? This is the story of humanhood and this is the story of the human race. Because of our spiritual sonship, however, we can make the transition from being under the law to being under the Christ. Life then is no longer lived under the law of matter or mind: life is then lived under the Christian rule of Grace.

Can you understand what it would mean to go through life under a Grace that would feed, clothe, and house you, that would prevent illness and accidents, and if they occurred, immediately heal them? How would it be to go through life, knowing that you no longer needed to take thought for your life and that you were living under a Grace that could bring forth for you the heritage of heaven? Can you for a moment imagine living in the spiritual kingdom under *My* peace in which you would live "not by might, nor by power, but by my spirit"?[1] Can you conceive of life lived with a divine Presence going before you to make straight the way and to prepare mansions for you? That is the life the Master proclaimed and taught, and the life he promised to those who follow his teachings. Such a life is possible, but how can the transition be made?

From the very beginning of modern metaphysics, over a hundred years ago, there have been those whose lives have been changed, remolded, and made new by these teachings. Strangely enough, however, in the same metaphysical movements where some have experienced miraculous changes, others, after years of study, will say that it has not benefited them at all. They have had the same truth, the same books, the same teachers, and yet nothing has happened. Truth operates equally for all those who dedicate themselves to the practice of truth, but there must be the practice. That is what separates those who are attaining spiritual living from those who are not. There were few who attained in Jesus' time, and not many more now seem willing to undertake the work of knowing the truth. It is much easier to say, "Oh, God is good," or "God is love," or "God is present," and let it go at that, but repeating words or clichés never works.

As a human being, you have no dominion whatsoever. You are acted upon by weather, climate, and food, and if you want to accept it, even by the stars above you. This is not living by the Spirit. To live under Grace, you must consciously negate the laws of the world and the world's dominion over you, and by an activity of consciousness become aware of the law of God operating in your experience.

62

What I have been telling you is based on a very early unfoldment in my work in which I saw that nothing could happen to me except through my consciousness. God could be filling all space around me, and yet not one bit of God could touch my life unless I consciously opened my consciousness to receive Him. In Isaiah, it is clearly stated, "Thou wilt keep him in perfect peace, whose mind is stayed on thee."[2] That is how you find your peace—by keeping your mind stayed on God. God will not do it: it is keeping your mind stayed on God that brings the activity of God into your experience.

"Lean not unto thine own understanding. In all thy ways acknowledge him."[3] Again it is you! You must acknowledge that God governs your day, God governs your purse, God governs your business, God governs your household, God governs your relationships with all mankind. You must bring God into your experience by a conscious act of your consciousness.

To "pray without ceasing"[4] is just another way of keeping your mind stayed on God and acknowledging Him in all your ways. Many passages in the Bible indicate that in proportion as you dwell "in the secret place of the most High,"[5] none of the evils of the world can come nigh your dwelling place. In spite of God's omnipresence, a thousand can fall at your left and ten thousand at your right, but it will not come nigh the dwelling place of the person who dwells and lives consciously in the realization of God's presence, God's power, and God's grace.

If you are to make the transition from being a person whose life is not God-governed to one whose life is God-governed, there is a price to be paid. I can tell you that for the first year or two the price is high and the way is hard. It means consciously remembering the Presence from morning to night.

Making the Word of God a Conscious Part of Your Activity

Whatever your field of activity, there may be difficulties, and often these difficulties are beyond your capacity to meet. Does this make life hopeless? It makes it hopeless only for the atheist. Scripture reveals: "He performeth the thing that is appointed for me.[6] . . . The Lord will perfect that which concerneth me.[7] . . . Greater is he that is in you, than he that is in the world."[8]

Some of you may say, "I have not been able to prove that." But have you been obeying Scripture in living by the word of God? If you have, the moment a problem comes to you that causes any concern, immediately there would flash into your thought, "I am not alone in this, and I do not have to meet it alone. There is a He within me that is greater than this problem. The kingdom of God is within me; the allness of God is within me; and the very place whereon I stand is holy ground because the presence of God is here." Then comes that relaxing from human strain and that feeling of being picked up by the Infinite Invisible, by the Presence that is always within you.

The moment you begin to live in and through the word of God by making it a conscious part of your daily activity, your life begins to change. Then the Spirit of God is dwelling in you because by an act of your own consciousness you have brought It out of dormancy into life. You have brought God into your life by your acknowledgment that the kingdom of God is within you, that there is a He within you that is greater than any problem in the world, and that God sent to you His son, who dwells with you and is within you.

Even the Master said, "I can of mine own self do nothing."[9] But the Father within, the Infinite Invisible that God planted in

64

you in the beginning, "before Abraham was,"[10] makes it possible for you to do all things and for all things to be done through you. Nothing is impossible to the Christ. Where is the Christ? It is the Spirit of God in you. Nothing is impossible to It.

If you become egotistical, however, and believe that you of your own self can accomplish the great things of life, you will fail. Something will happen to prove to you that you are not quite so great as you may have thought you were. But as long as you can abide in the word of God, realizing that there is an infinite Presence within you, this Presence will go before you to smooth out every rough place in your path.

Foundation Stones for a Life of Prayer

To begin your journey on the spiritual path, you must have at least three periods a day for prayer, meditation, and inner communion. Eventually you will increase these periods to from twenty to thirty each day. True, some of them may be one minute or even as short as ten, twenty, or thirty seconds, but they will bring the realization:

Thank You, Father, for omnipotence, omnipresence, and omniscience. Thank You, Father, that besides You there is no other power. There is no power of destruction, no power of time or place, no power of age, no power of sin, no power of disease, no power of the carnal mind—just no power but the power of God's grace here where I am.

One minute of this twenty times a day would change your life so rapidly that soon your friends and relatives would not recognize you. But that is where the difficulty comes in. You intend to do it twenty times a day and forget eighteen times. That makes no difference, since tomorrow you will probably forget it only seven-

65

teen times. By the end of the week, you will not forget so often. Then when the fruitage begins to roll in, you will never let it get away from you.

Through these short meditations, you have the assurance in the midst of your normal day's living that you are continuing in and under God's grace. To practice meditations of only a few seconds' duration, you do not have to close your eyes, nor do you even have to sit down. You can pray while in your office working, at home, cooking or housecleaning, or while you are driving your car. Regardless of what you are doing with your body, you can give ten seconds to this:

I in God, and God in me. Where I am, God is.

That is enough! Another hour:

"Underneath are the everlasting arms."[11] *Here where I am, God is.*

And that meditation, too, is enough! Another hour:

I live, not by might nor by power, but by God's grace. I can rest in the assurance of that Grace.

Another hour you may look at a tree and realize:

Day and night, the life of God is animating that tree, and even though it seems barren at this moment, the very activity of God is the assurance that in due season there will be fruit.

So, too, if at the moment I appear to be barren of health, wealth, or opportunity, I realize that the presence of God in me is the assurance that in due season I, too, will bear fruit richly.

Never less than once in every hour must there be these ten seconds of conscious remembrance:

I in God, and God in me. I live by Grace, not by might nor by power. So let me be still and know that I in the midst of me am God.

Just ten seconds now and then are enough to keep you consciously in the atmosphere of God, to serve to fulfill Scripture in your experience, and to maintain the contact between you and your Source. Wherever you are, you must have a ten-second period every little while to remember:

The grace of God is upon me. I have meat to share with all who are here, spiritual meat, spiritual bread, and those who are accepting it will never hunger. I can give to those in this room spiritual water, and those who accept it will never thirst again. "I and my Father are one,"[12] *and the Father is pouring the allness of the Godhead through me to you and to this world.*

Those of us who are trying to live the life of prayer engage in all the natural and normal activities that are a part of everyday living, and we do all things that for the time being are necessary. We eat our breakfast, luncheon, and dinner because they are as much a part of our day's life as is our daily bath. Then we dismiss these routine activities from our mind, so that the rest of our time can be spent in prayer. This does not mean that we are praying all the time: it means that we are in prayer.

To be in prayer means to be in a listening attitude, in an inner stillness, not cluttered up with outside noises. Then if the Voice should speak, we are able to hear It. The noises outside or the jet planes flying overhead need not annoy us because inside there is

67

a part of us unmoved by those outer things and able to listen for the Voice, even in the clamor of the world.

Practicing the Presence

Early in your experience, you will learn that in order to live a life of prayer, it is necessary to practice the presence of God, consciously to make an effort to keep God in consciousness. Beginning in the morning with the recognition that this is the day the Lord has made and stopping periodically to remember some passage of Scripture is building the temple with truth. Except truth build the temple, it will not be a spiritual temple. So begin your day with the truth that God governs this day just as He governs the activity of the sun, moon, stars, and planets. As He governs the time and the tides, so God governs your day from waking to sleeping, and throughout the night.

At breakfast time, again there is a momentary pause just to say, "Thank You, Father, the earth is full of Your bounty." Not only do you thank the Father that your table is full—that alone would be a selfish kind of prayer—but you realize that "the earth is the Lord's, and the fulness thereof,"[13] and all that the Father has belongs to every son and daughter. Upon leaving your home in the morning, remember that the Presence goes before you to "make the crooked places straight"[14] and to build mansions for you.

Later some problem may be presented to you greater than your ability to solve, and that is an opportunity for another ten seconds just to remember, "He performeth the thing that is appointed for me. . . . The Lord will perfect that which concerneth me." The weight drops off your shoulders; the responsibility drops away from you; and you know that you are not building this temple alone: God is building it for you. "Except the Lord keep the city, the watchman waketh but in vain."[15] So you take ten seconds for remembering: the Lord is keeping the watch; He is performing that which is given you to do. Relaxing in this way, you are giving Him an opportunity to come through and take over.

Driving on the road, you will need that ten seconds to remember:

There is only one Being on the road. There may be a million drivers, but there is only one Being, and that Being is God, sitting at every wheel, the only driver of every car.

If you do not consciously remember that, you are not bringing it into your experience. It is the conscious recognition and the conscious acknowledgment of it that makes it demonstrable.

Just as you begin your day by knowing the truth, so you retire at night with an activity of truth in your consciousness which changes the nature of your night's rest.

I am not going to sleep as a human being. I am resting in the divine consciousness of the Truth I have embodied during these many years. I am going to rest consciously aware of the word of God, alive and alert in me, whether asleep or awake.

As many times a day as you can think of it—later you will do it without consciously thinking of it—blink the eyes, if it is only for a second, and remember Omnipresence, Omnipotence, or Omniscience. Every time you remember the word "Omniscience," you will know that you do not have to tell God what you need or where you want to be. All you have to do is to think the one word "Omniscience," and you will instantaneously know that God already knows. Every time you think of Omnipresence, you will know that whatever you were thinking of is already present.

When you think of Omnipotence, you will know that there is no power that can deprive you of life eternal, of harmony, peace,

Grace, and spiritual abundance. The very word "Omnipotence" is the assurance to you that there is no power but God. God could not be all-power and there be a power of evil to fear. You can live a life of prayer with one word or with a brief scriptural citation entertained in consciousness.

The first month or two of a life of prayer may be difficult, but after a couple of months of this practice, a person could no more go through a fifteen-minute period without some conscious realization of God than he could go fifteen minutes without breathing. It would be impossible. Living in this attitude, you will be living by Grace.

DAILY PREPARATION

You can be of no greater help to anyone than the measure of truth established in your consciousness. Before you leave your home in the morning to go about your activities, whether they be marketing, shopping, or business, you must undertake a daily work to remind yourself that you have "died" to your human sense and have been reborn through the Word. Your consciousness is constituted of the word of God, and as you go out into the world, you carry God's grace everywhere you walk.

All who enter your consciousness during the day—whether they be storekeepers, customers, clients, patients, students, friends, or enemies—must feel the power of God which is stored up within you through your years of opening yourself to the word of God which is truth and which now constitutes your very being. God's truth is the fiber of your being, reaching even to the bones, the marrow, and the joints. Every bit of you is filled with God. Even your body is the temple of God, a storehouse of God's power and God's grace.

You learn never to leave your home without a conscious realiza-

70

tion of truth. When you have completed this, you can sit quietly and wait in the receptive atmosphere created by your knowing of the truth until you feel the seal of God upon you. If it does not come at first, do not let that disturb you. Be thorough about the work, bringing to it all that you can remember of the principles of The Infinite Way.

In this morning preparation, you must provide a minute for consciously releasing all those who have given offense, whether it is against you, democracy, justice, or the word of God. Set them free! Release them! Be willing that they be forgiven without penalty. Be sure that you are praying that God open the minds and the souls and the consciousness of those whom you call enemies.

All this must be included in your daily preparation. It cannot be neglected, for only what you put into it comes out as demonstration. The important thing to know is that you expect this knowing of the truth to be effective because it is the word of God entertained in your consciousness. That "word of God is quick, and powerful, and sharper than any two-edged sword."[16]

Whether the problem is some form of sin, disease, lack, limitation, or unhappiness, your prayer work must include the realization that this that is binding you is not power. It must include the realization that you are not invoking a God-power to destroy a sin or a disease. The truth you are realizing is that nothing is power but God. What then can hinder you?

SENDING THE WORD BEFORE YOU

Whatever is entertained in your consciousness is known to your neighbors. Intuitively they can tell whether your consciousness is a blessing, a curse, or a vacuum doing nothing of a constructive nature and nothing of a negative nature—just vegetating. You know when you are in the presence of a positive person, whether

71

he is positive for good or positive on the evil side, and you know when you are in the presence of a wishy-washy sort that is neither good nor evil, but just going along for the ride.

Your responsibility as a neighbor is to be a positive influence for good. You do not have to project yourself into his human affairs. You do not have to be his adviser, nor do you need to proselyte and try to bring him into some teaching for which he has not been prepared. You are a positive influence for good only in proportion as your consciousness is active in truth, filled with the truth that you are consciously uttering silently, sacredly, secretly.

You do not have to tell anyone that you are praying for him or that you hope to be a blessing to him. Be satisfied if God's grace touches him without your getting any personal credit for it. Let God have the glory. Be a good steward of the word of God, not one who just hoards it up in the mind and lets it rest there. Put it out to be of use.

Do not leave home in the morning without sending the Word before you:

Wherever I am, the word of God is, for it constitutes my newborn consciousness and, therefore, is a benediction and a blessing. It is a healer; it is bread, wine, meat, water, and supply unto all who touch it.

Your consciousness is as infinite as God because God constitutes your consciousness, and God is infinite. All who are embraced in your consciousness are embraced in the law of God, if you know it and consciously remember it.

These truths consciously realized before you leave home in the morning change the nature of your day. As pointed out before, a person living as a human being is subject to chance, accident, or change, subject to every wind that blows: infection, contagion, unemployment, lack, limitation. Whatever is in the air, zoom, the human being falls victim to it. Why? Because his mind is a vacuum, and he picks up every thought that blows. Not so the mystical student, the spiritual student! Not so those who live and move and have their being in the word of God! You cannot let your mind be a vacuum. You cannot let it be acted upon by those who want to do you *good,* and those who want to *do* you good. This is not a lazy man's work, nor is it a lazy way of life.

Keep the word of God in your mind, in your soul, and in your heart. If you abide in the Word and let the Word abide in you consciously, you will be one of those who give the benediction, the blessing, not of yourself, but by the grace of God through the truth which you embody in your consciousness, and which you never forget.

And so, in the morning before you leave your home and at night before you go to bed, lesson number one, the first step, very short, very sweet, very gentle: acknowledge God within. The rest of the flight of stairs leads all the way up to heaven.

· 7 ·

Planting and Cultivating
the Seed

WITH THE CONTINUED PRACTICE of the presence of God comes a
steady lessening of personal responsibility. An inner quiet, a peace,
and a joy develop which make contemplative meditation easier.
The practice of the Presence begins to remold your entire consciousness so that instead of your living your own life or being
dependent on your own wisdom, education, or physical strength,
you are now drawing on this untapped invisible Source which is
available to every person in the degree that he knows the truth.

Throughout the day as you acknowledge that regardless of the
name or nature of your problem there is a He within you greater
than any problem that faces you, you relax in Him. Eventually the
day comes when you can say, "I am not living my own life. I am
living, yes, but I am not striving or struggling: Christ is living my
life, this Spirit of God in me, this spiritual Presence." There is an
awareness of Something.

Practicing the presence of God leads to meditation, and meditation leads to the actual contact with God and an inner assurance
of His presence. Then you are praying the prayer that enables you
to be in the inner sanctuary within yourself and there tabernacle
with God.

The Invisible Life-Force in Operation

Think for a moment of a garden. To bring forth fruitage, seeds must be planted. You may keep the seeds stored away for days, weeks, months, or years, and nothing happens to them. But the moment you place those seeds in the ground and provide them with the necessary rain, sun, air, and temperature, something happens. The seed breaks open, takes root, sends shoots up through the ground, and eventually becomes a plant or tree, bearing flowers or fruit. The point is that something happened to that seed when it was placed in its natural environment, the ground.

If you could look down into the ground, using the most powerful of magnifying glasses and time-photography, you would observe the seed breaking open, but you could not see what made it break open. You might see it take root, but you have no way of seeing what causes it to take root. You could observe it growing up through the ground, but could you see what is forcing it up? Whatever that force is, it is invisible to human sight. No one has ever seen what causes the seed to become a full-grown tree or what brings forth the fruit. That is an invisible process. Scripture tells us that all things that are formed are formed of things that are not seen, and that which is not seen is the invisible Something, the invisible Presence, the invisible Power.

Consider the sun, the moon, the stars, the planets and their movements. No one has ever seen what causes these movements and perpetuates them. Why? Because the Force or Power is invisible. It is invisible, and yet It is power; It is invisible, and yet It is present. Whether down in the ground or up in the sky, this invisible Presence and Power is functioning. Moreover, It is an intelligent Presence and Power. When It operates through a banana tree, It produces bananas. When It acts upon the tides, It

75

moves them in and out, thus far and no further. It maintains the sun, the stars, and the moon in their orbits, generation after generation. It is a very loving Presence and Power, because It can always be depended upon to continue Its activity through rain, storm, sleet, or in periods of peace and war.

Then why is there such chaos in the world today and why are people so disturbed? The reason is found by looking at so simple a thing as a seed. Just as you could keep seeds in your hands forever without their bearing fruit, because they have been kept out of their native element, the ground, so you can keep yourself in sin, disease, lack, limitation, warfare, or even in death, just by keeping yourself out of your native element, the invisible Substance.

According to Scripture, "In him we live, and move, and have our being."[1] Swimming in an ocean, flying in a plane, even on a battlefield, wherever you are, you live, move, and have your being in God. You are planted in Him, rooted and grounded in Him. You cannot remove yourself from God, because God is your natural habitat. If you wish the seed of the truth of God's omnipresence to bear fruit, you must take it into your withinness and there remember:

The entire air that surrounds me is an ocean of God, and it fills me outside and inside. I live and move and have my being in this ocean of God, in this sea of love and wisdom. I am in God, and God is in me.

Your conscious knowing of this truth provides the soil or atmosphere that brings the activity of this invisible Presence and Power into expression in your life. You can either avoid good by not acknowledging Him in all your ways or, through steadfastly abiding in the truth of God's presence, you can experience safety, security, protection, justice, equity, and equality. But no one can bring these things to you, not even God. You, yourself, must live consciously in Him, and He will establish you in all your ways. Do you think that you can do this? No, not you of yourself. It is the divine Presence within you that does the works.

MEDITATION PROVIDES THE SOIL

If the Spirit of God has not touched you, you will not be conscious of the indwelling Presence. Open your consciousness and feel the peace that passes understanding, right here where you are. Consciously remember that the son of God abides in you, and this son of God is your meat, your bread, your supply, your safety, your income forever. Your consciousness of this indwelling spiritual Presence is your eternal supply, *your* consciousness.

To meditate or pray correctly, it is necessary to understand at least a few spiritual principles of life in order that these may be embraced in the meditation. A meditation that has in it no conscious awareness of a spiritual principle can lead to a mental stillness without any spiritual fruitage. For this reason you must know why you are meditating and you must also know what principles to bring into your meditation.

There are the ten-second meditations to be used as reminders. There are also longer meditations of perhaps ten minutes' duration for the contemplation of truth and the actual communion with the Father within. A communion has in it something of a back-and-forth nature. You are virtually saying to the Father:

Thank You, Father, that Your grace is upon me. Thank You, Father, that You have given me Your peace. Of my own self, I could not have faith, hope, or confidence. Whatever measure of these I have is the gift of Your grace within me.

77

Then there is a pause, a listening for the inner Voice. If you persist in this way of life, eventually the Father will speak in some such manner as this:

Son, you are ever with Me; *all that* I *have is yours. You are* My *son,* My *heir.* I *have been with you since before time began. Do you not know that* I *will be with you unto the end of the world, that* I *will never leave you nor forsake you?*

Turn and recognize Me. *Acknowledge* Me, *and you will find* Me, *even in hell. If you walk through any valley,* I *will not leave you. Turn within; seek* Me! *Realize and acknowledge* Me *in the midst of you, and* I *will turn death into life, age into youth, lack into abundance. Only abide in this Word; let* Me *consciously abide in you. Whither do you think you can flee from* My *Spirit?*

If the Spirit of God dwells in you and you have been led to a spiritual way of life, you will never be able to forget either the ten-second meditations or the ten-minute contemplative meditations; you will be as unable to go through the hours of the day and night without the conscious remembrance of the presence of God as you would be unable to go without food or drink. As food and drink are essential to "the natural man,"[2] so the conscious awareness of the presence of God is essential to the spiritual man. Spiritual food is more important to the son of God than is material food.

The Spiritual Life Is a Life of Sharing

Always the first reminder must be: What have I in my house? What have I in my consciousness? Then you can have ten, fifteen, twenty, or thirty minutes of contemplative meditation, just going within and finding what you already have in your house. There is no time, I can assure you, for thinking about what you may lack or what you are missing. There is only time for the remembrance of what you already have.

Just think! You are living: you have life; you have consciousness; you have intelligence; you have reasoning power. All this has been given to you as the gift of God. Acknowledge it! Acknowledge that you have reasoning power, thinking power, intelligence, wisdom, guidance, direction, and that they are yours as the gift of God. Acknowledge that you have an inner substance, an inner life, an inner truth, an inner grace.

Notice how this changes the direction of your thought from the "natural man" who is always wanting something or seeking to get something to being the spiritual son of God who is always saying, "Ask of me, and I can give you. I can give you the peace that passes understanding. I can share with you the indwelling Christ-peace that the Father has given me." Observe how this reverses the trend of your life.

The spiritual man is not only always receiving, but sharing, because he cannot lay up these treasures "where moth and rust doth corrupt."[3] Spiritual treasures cannot be laid up. They are always in expression. They are always flowing out. You bring them to your home. You bring them to your business. You let them flow to your enemy as well as to your friend: "I share Christ's blessings with friend and foe and hope that my foe may have the spiritual capacity to receive what I offer."

In your home realize: "I bring to this home living waters. I bring to this home divine Love. I bring to this home the grace of God." Think what is pouring out through you to this world, and then ask yourself how many years it will be until there is peace on earth. There never has been peace on earth, because everyone has come here looking for it, and so few have ever come to bring it. If you bring peace to this earth, it will be there, but if you, like the "natural man," come looking for peace on earth, you will never

79

find it. It is not here until you bring it.

What have you in your consciousness? You have the peace that passes understanding. You can take it wherever you will, wherever you are, because in the Christ-presence there is fulfillment, and the Christ dwells in you.

The indwelling Christ is the fulfillment. Where the Christ is, there is peace. So I *bring peace to my body;*I *bring peace and quiet to my mind;* I *bring peace, quiet, love, and abundance to this home and all who are therein.* I *bring to you the grace of God.*My *peace, the Christ-peace, give* I *unto you.*

THE PRESENCE BECOMES AN EXPERIENCE

As prayer and meditation become increasingly a way of life, you discover that something of an unusual nature takes place. The kingdom of God, this very presence of God that is within you, makes Itself known to you. It either speaks to you in plain language or It announces Itself in a feeling of the Presence or in an assurance. In one way or another, a moment comes when, instead of talking about the Presence or seeking It, all of a sudden you feel It. There It is! Before, you have heard of It with "the hearing of the ear."[4] Now, you experience It.

Usually, it is of such brief duration that you wonder whether it really happened or whether it was your imagination. It was not your imagination at all. It really happened, and it will happen again and again. Eventually, that brief moment will be two brief moments. Many have had the experience of being able consciously to commune with the Spirit within them for hours and hours, and sometimes for days and days, and It never leaves.

There does come an end to the experience of actual communion, however, and then you go back into the world and do your daily tasks, but do them better than before and with much more love, with much less of judgment and criticism, and certainly with a freedom from fear. But you get lonesome for that Presence and sometimes, when It does not come back as quickly as you would like, you become very unhappy.

With patience and continued meditation, however, It does return, and eventually It returns at will. It comes back at any moment that you want to blink your eyes. As a matter of fact, it almost seems as if there are only brief periods when It is absent from you. Even then It is not really absent, just in the background. Whenever a need appears for It, you can bring It into conscious awareness by reaching into your own consciousness. There is nothing outside in the world for you to seek or gain. Everything there is, is right now within your own consciousness, and you learn to turn within two or three times every day just for the realization:

The allness of God is within me. Whatever I have been seeking in life I will now find. It is in my own being and it will come forward.

This attitude leads to a contact with your Source and to an actual communion with God. During this period, which sometimes is a very long one in your life, going on often for years, it would almost seem as if you were denying the truth that you and the Father are one, because there is always a "you" and there is always the Father within to whom you are reaching out for assurance and reassurance, with whom you are communing, and there is that Father within who responds. Whether or not that response is in words is not important, because in one way or another, the assurance is given, and experiences take place in your life for which you are not personally or humanly responsible.

Through practicing the Presence, you have reached into medi-

81

tation and from meditation into that inner communion with God, an actual living with This that is within you, talking to you much more than you ever talk to It, letting you know by Its presence that you have nothing to fear in this world. And this is prayer.

PLANTING YOURSELF IN GOD

You can change your life in the same way that you change the life of a seed when you plant it in the ground. No matter what the life of the seed may have been while you were carrying it in your pocket, it changes the moment it is planted in the ground. So does your life change the moment you plant yourself in Him. All you have to do, wherever you are, is to recognize:

Here where I am, God is. I swim in a sea of infinite Wisdom and Love. I soar up into the atmosphere, still surrounded by the everlasting Life and the everlasting Love, which are the nature of God. I cannot escape from His everlasting arms which are underneath and around me. I live, and move, and have my being in Him. I rest in Him.

By the grace of God, the earth is filled with His goodness, and the air and the seas with His bounty. By Grace, the heavens and the earth declare the fullness and the infinite abundance of His glory. Those who do not experience that fulfillment either will not plant the seeds or they will not cultivate them. To whatever extent a person is not flourishing, it is not the fault of God: it is the fault of his not planting and cultivating the seed of truth within himself. If you plant a seed of truth within your consciousness this moment and cultivate it faithfully, it will spring up into newness of life. Do not plant it and go away and neglect it: cultivate it. Day by day, know this truth:

The kingdom of God is established within me. I am living, not only surrounded by air, but surrounded by the life, the love, and the wisdom of God. I am swimming in an ocean of God; I am soaring and flying like the birds in the atmosphere of God. Consciously, I have God dwelling in me, and I can do all things through God that dwells in me and I in Him, for we are one.

God is the invisible presence of Intelligence and Love, and this infinite invisible presence of Wisdom and Love is within me and without me. I am in It, and It is in me. Where I am, It is; where It is, I am, for we are inseparable, indivisible, one.

This is a form of contemplative meditation, and it constitutes the activity of cultivating the seed of truth that we plant within ourselves.

After students have been studying The Infinite Way for a year or two, they set aside not less than three or four periods each day, periods of five, ten, or fifteen minutes for the purpose of consciously dwelling in God and consciously letting God dwell in them. Then the rest of the day, they live their lives, tend to their business or profession, whatever it may be, the same as everyone else. The only difference between them and the rest of the world is that they now have the Spirit of God dwelling in them because they have consciously brought it about.

No one can give you heaven permanently. This must be your act. It is you who live with yourself twenty-four hours a day, and the way in which you live with yourself determines the nature of your life. It is never too late, and it is really never too early. The sooner you begin, the sooner you are living in the atmosphere of God. Between now and ten thousand years from now, you can in any moment choose to live in His Spirit.

Plant the seed of truth in your consciousness and begin daily to nourish it with brief periods of practicing the Presence which means a conscious remembrance of living in God and of life by Grace. Stop fighting life; stop chasing after God; and God will come right up to you.

Be still! In quietness and in confidence, I give you peace and rest. Rest! Rest! In quietness and in confidence, I am with you. In quietness and in confidence, you will feel that My peace is upon you. My peace give I unto you. My grace is yours. My grace is your sufficiency.

Put up your sword! You need not fight. Relax, rest! Eat of My meat: you will never hunger! Drink of My water: you will never thirst! Relax in Me, and let Me abide in you. Consciously rest in Me.

I am the resurrection, even to raising up that old dead body into newness of life. I am the resurrection that restores the lost years of the locusts. Only do not fight! Put up your sword. Son, I am ever with you, and all that I have is yours.

I give you this as a seed of truth. You plant it in your consciousness; you nurture it; you feed it; you remember it day by day— quietly, peacefully, joyously—and in due season, the fruitage will appear.

· 8 ·

Let the Spirit Bear Witness

WHEN YOU MAKE CONTACT with the Spirit of God that is within you, you bring into your experience the divine Power and Presence. The work of The Infinite Way is attaining the conscious awareness of that Presence. When you realize that It is "closer . . . than breathing,"* you stop the search for It in heaven or in holy mountains, and you begin to rest. In that resting you open out a way for the Spirit to announce Itself and perform Its function.

Was not the ministry of the Master the healing of the sick, the raising of the dead, the feeding of the hungry, the forgiving of the sinner, and the overcoming of the discords and inharmonies of life, regardless of the forms in which these discords may have appeared? Is not the Christ-ministry today primarily one of overcoming what the Master called "this world," whether it appears as sin, temptation, false appetite, lack, or limitation?

For most persons, it is a simple thing to acknowledge that there is an indwelling Christ, but it is difficult to prove It, to manifest It, or to bring It forth. But this will follow if, and only if, something within you says, "Yes," when you hear or read of the

*Alfred Tennyson.

85

Christ-presence within. It was the Master's awareness and conviction of that Presence that did the miracle works of which you read.

All those engaged in spiritual healing know that healing takes place only when they come to the end of the prayer or treatment and have an inner release or feeling: "It is done"; or "God is on the scene." Prayer or treatment that consists only of words or thoughts, no matter how sublime or how true they may be, is ineffectual and brings forth no response from the Divine. Only the prayer or treatment that transcends words and thoughts and attains an actual contact with the Spirit brings fruitage.

I am not saying that you should do away with prayers or treatments that consist of words or thoughts. Heaven forbid! These are the tools you use; these are the instruments you use to ascend above them. Regardless of the nature of your prayer or treatment, it must be only for the purpose of reaching a place in consciousness where the words and thoughts stop and the Spirit Itself takes over.

If the prayer of words and thoughts itself were power, there would be no such thing today as seeking a spiritual path or finding some way to bring spiritual power to earth, because in every religion, denomination, and sect, there are prayers and treatments enough to swamp the world with good. But if you let your treatment embody all the truth that you possibly can bring to remembrance, and then, at the end of it, pause and wait for the Spirit to be upon you, you will find the real meaning of prayer, and you will discover the source and secret of spiritual healing.

"Stay in the City"

In the Revised Standard Version of the Bible, there is a remarkable passage in next to the last verse in Luke. As the Master is leaving the disciples, he says to them, "Stay in the city!" Do not go out and try to proselyte; do not go out and preach; do not go out and pray; do not go out! "Stay in the city."

You are taught to remain in prayer until you receive power from on High. The Master quoted from Isaiah, "The Spirit of the Lord is upon me, because he hath anointed me."[1] Even though you may know all the truth in a book and know the Scriptures, do not believe that this constitutes being anointed of God. You are anointed of God only when you feel the Presence.

Unless in some way there comes an assurance within you that there is Something more than you, your prayer is ineffective. When an inner sense of peace descends upon you, a release from concern, an assurance that *I* will never leave you, that *I* am with you, this can be the end of your particular prayer. Then whatsoever things you ask will be done. Also, by virtue of that Spirit, you will know enough not to ask for material things or for material good.

What do you need to pray for? Nothing! What do you believe God is withholding from you? Nothing! Then why are you closing your eyes in prayer? Why, except that you may receive the grace of God, that His Spirit may be upon you, that you may be healed physically, mentally, morally, financially, whatever the need may be. You would have no other reason for going into prayer.

As you close your eyes in prayer, God knows that it is for the purpose of being an instrument through which His grace reaches your consciousness. Then when you are still enough, let His voice come thundering into your consciousness or enter gently and peaceably, because the all-knowing Consciousness knows that you are in prayer to receive divine Grace.

I am here in the silence to receive Thy peace, to receive Thy kingdom, Thy grace.

Abide in that stillness, quietness, and peace until the Spirit of God descends and inwardly you feel a release from the problem, a release from fear and anxiety. Then, in Its season, God's grace takes the form of a healing, of an uplifting, of supplying, of a happier human relationship, something very tangible.

Prayer is the ability to enter the silence without a problem, just for the joy of communion with God, for the experience of coming to know God aright. Prayer is an attitude of self-surrender and an altitude of consciousness that rises above wanting, desiring, or achieving, and becomes a communion with the Source of life. When that communion takes place and the inner response comes, the benediction of the Lord has been received.

The miracle is not just that a pain has been dissolved, a disease has disappeared, or an unhappiness has given way to happiness. It goes further than this. The world has been overcome. The source of evil has been eliminated. These constant meditations which result in the inner contact gradually lead to the dissolving of problems, not merely *a* problem; but one after another, and sometimes, two by two, the problems that constitute the world disappear.

LAYING THE AXE AT THE ROOT

A problem can exist only in what is called the universal human mind, and it finds outlet through an individual. If you refuse to let it flow out from you, the problem is dead. Problems are but the universal belief in two powers, and the very moment you acknowledge this and accept God as Omnipotence, you are destroying the problem in the only place where it existed, and that is in the universal human mind.

In ancient days, the source of evil was given the name "devil." Devil is not and never was a person. Devil or evil is something of an impersonal nature. It may appear as sin; it may appear as

88

juvenile delinquency; it may appear as false appetite; it may appear as an incurable disease; it may appear as poverty; it may appear as death. But whatever the name or nature, you are faced with only one evil, for which we use Paul's designation, "the carnal mind,"[2] or a term such as "appearance." The discord is not a physical entity or identity: it is an appearance, the product of the carnal mind, the belief in two powers.

Instead of concerning yourself with the specific nature of a problem, realize instantly, "Ah, this is my old friend Satan, carnal mind, appearance." Then recognize that since only what is of God is power, the appearance or suggestion has no power, no law, no continuity, and nothing to sustain it.

If you could accept God as Omnipotence, you would just turn your back on any and every phase of error and walk away. But most persons are not able to do this. Instead, they argue with it; they fight it; they even pray about it. Once you have recognized God as Omnipotence, however, you have nothing to pray about. Your prayer then is one of communion with God and a rejoicing in the Spirit. It is the prayer of recognition, the prayer of tabernacling with God, not asking something of God or trying to use God as a power.

When you understand God as Omnipotence, you are able to turn away from evil in any form with the words, "You could have no power over me unless it came from God. Besides God, there is no power; and this Power is not more up in the sky than it is right here where I am."

When you are faced with what appears to be an evil and you would meet it spiritually, you must first know that evil is not a power. You must also understand that you are not trying to change human evil into human good. You are not trying to exchange one human condition for another human condition. Be watchful of this! When you are faced with sin, you must not try to change it

89

to purity. When you are faced with disease, you must not try to change it to health. When you are faced with death, you must not try to change it to life. When you are faced with loss, you must not try to change it to gain.

If you are not to do this, then what are you to do? You must realize that neither human loss nor human gain is of any importance. If you had the best health in the world one minute, there would not be a thing to prevent you from dropping dead the next minute. In facing an appearance of evil, you do not try to change it into good. You realize the nonpower and illusory nature of both human evil and human good, and your prayer is, "Let me bear witness to spiritual truth, spiritual harmony, and spiritual good." This is rising above the pairs of opposites.

You cannot return to the Garden of Eden until you have risen above both good and evil. As long as you are merely trying to exchange evil for good or turn evil into good, you are not in paradise because, in spite of the degree of good, it can again become evil. Have you not seen people struggle to attain a million dollars and then end up with nothing? Have you not seen athletes and health faddists struggle to build themselves up to what they think is a perfect physical body and then wreck themselves? Have you not seen people who strive to be righteous pulled down and destroyed physically, mentally, morally, or financially, in spite of their so-called righteousness?

Evil cannot be overcome by might or by power. There is no such thing as victory over evil, except as there is an overturning and an overturning "until he come whose right it is."[3] As you learn how to face disease without fighting or trying to overcome it, sitting beside it in the silence until the Spirit within you bears witness, then health of a permanent nature that does not have to be gained again and again is established. In the same way, when false appetites are overcome by will power, by fighting them, many times it does not prove to be lasting, but when overcome spiritually, there remains a permanent blessing.

On the human level, taking a "resist not"[4] attitude would mean merely to give your adversary the opportunity to take advantage of you. On the spiritual path, this is not true. When you undertake to meet problems of health, morals, finances, or any form of evil that opposes you—injustice, inequality—resisting, if you can, the desire to change evil into good and are willing to bear witness to the spiritual Presence and Power, harmony evolves.

GOOD COMES IN TERMS OF OUR CONDITIONING

Spiritual harmony comes as infinite perfection, but the degree that you experience is proportionate to your conditioned mind.* Every person has been conditioned somewhat by his ancestry, his nationality, his religion, a great deal more by his education, and finally by his personal experience in life. Therefore, when he turns to Spirit, it is more than likely that the grace of God will come through in some form conditioned by his state of consciousness.

God knows nothing of disease; God knows nothing of a heart that has to beat at some prescribed rate. Be assured that if God knew anything about such things, the heart would be beating correctly all the time. Nothing is outside the power of God. But you have been conditioned to an idea of how fast or slow the heart should beat, and so when God voices harmony of body, it is only natural that you interpret it in that rate of heartbeat or that degree of temperature.

Sometimes persons who cannot sleep or do not sleep enough turn to the Spirit and find afterward that they sleep eight or nine

*See the author's "The Unconditioned Mind," in *The Thunder of Silence* (New York: Harper & Row, 1961).

hours. I suppose they might imagine that God intends that they should sleep that long, but let it be understood clearly that it is not necessary to sleep at all, as far as God is concerned. God neither slumbers nor sleeps, nor does His image and likeness. Therefore, if you turn to the Spirit and find yourself sleeping eight or nine hours, it is because you have conditioned yourself to accept that as a normal amount of sleep, whereas there have been many persons who have accomplished great things who have been able to get along with much less sleep. If God intended that they should have eight hours' sleep, they would have it. However, they conditioned themselves and knew that they could function with less sleep, and they did.

When good unfolds, strangely enough, it unfolds to one person as a luxurious automobile, another as a streamlined yacht, another as a brilliant diamond or a beautiful home. Why, if God is giving them His grace, should it not be that they all receive beautiful homes? No, they condition what comes to them by something latent in their consciousness. Nothing is impossible because their true nature is unconditioned mind, unconditioned Spirit, unconditioned Soul. In reality they are unconditioned consciousness, but the conditioning they have received creates a state of limitation for them. When they come to the spiritual path, they have to undo that conditioning. That is not easy. With every problem they have to retire within and realize: "God is. God is omnipresent where I am, and God is infinite, infinite good."

With every disease you have to remember consciously that disease is no part of God's will, and for that reason it has no power. Only what is ordained of God is power; only what is empowered of God is power. You have to train yourself to undo all that your parents, your church, and your schools have taught you until you come to the absolute conviction that God is all, and that the power of God is only good.

92

All the physiological changes that come with the passing of years should take place without pain, without discord, and without inharmony. Age has nothing to do with the body or with the calendar. It has to do with whether or not you believe that there is a regenerative process in you that is rebuilding you as fast as time can tear you down. How can there be old age for a person who acknowledges, "*I* will never leave you, even if you get to be one hundred twenty years. *I* am the health of your countenance"?

You cannot get along without some material food, but if you believe that food alone is maintaining you, you are withering, and eventually you will show it. You can do with far less food and be better fed, if part of your food is spiritual.

In the conscious realization of the Presence lies your entire salvation. The moment that this assurance of an inner benediction or Grace takes place, the Presence goes before you to "make the crooked places straight."[5] The Presence walks beside you and behind you. The Presence forgives your sins, heals your diseases, takes from you your lacks and your limitations. It must always be remembered, however, that the words or the repetition of words will not accomplish this. It must be the actual attainment of the Presence, and then you are endowed from on High.

· 9 ·

Two or More Gathered
Together

THROUGHOUT THE WORLD, there are groups of students on the spiritual path who meet together regularly—some daily, some weekly—and whether large or small they meet for one purpose only: to abide in God-consciousness. They have no motive other than to be a blessing and a benediction, and there is no possibility of selfish gain through such an activity or through such meetings.

Wherever two or more are gathered together for the purpose of God-realization, there is the temple of God, and God is in His temple. While it is true that "one on God's side is a majority,"* nevertheless it is also true that where there are two or more, that united consciousness brings forth great fruitage. "Where two or three are gathered together in my name, there am I in the midst of them."[1]

A specific work is necessary to establish a spiritual activity in a community. That work is not of a material nature: it is purely spiritual. In the quietness of your own home, in the park, or anywhere that you please, you can sit and silently do the work

*Wendell Phillips.

which will bear fruitage in a group activity and further fruitage in healing to those who attend these meetings.

Whenever such a meeting is to be held, you should undertake the spiritual work for its fruitage, whether that fruitage is to appear in the number of persons who are drawn to the meeting or whether it is to appear in the form of healing for those who are there. We are not so concerned with numbers as we are with attracting those who are seeking spiritual light and then giving them the fruitage after they have come.

Spiritual Preparation for Group Meetings

In undertaking spiritual work, you never follow a formula, nor use any set prayer or meditation. It must be inspirational, but it must cover and embrace the major principles which constitute the prayer work of a truly spiritual teaching. You must realize that those who enter the place where the meeting is held are not being attracted by a room, regardless of how beautiful it may be. They are being attracted by the consciousness of truth. As they enter the door, they enter the consciousness of your spiritual household, and therefore, everyone in the meeting enters the household of God as a guest, as a brother, a sister, a son, a daughter.

Divine consciousness, which is your consciousness and mine, enfolds all those who attend the meeting. Embraced in this consciousness of truth, God's grace permeates the being and touches the mind, soul, and body of each one. "Know ye not that ye are the temple of God . . . ?"[2] Those who enter the temple, which you are, are entering the temple of God and receive blessing, redeeming, raising up, and restoring. Your mind, imbued with truth, is a law of harmony, healing, health, happiness, peace, and prosperity.

I keep my mind stayed on God from rising in the morning until sleeping at night. Always there is some spiritual truth active in my consciousness, some scriptural passage kept alive within me. My mind is permeated with truth; it is constituted of truth; and all who enter the realm of my mind find truth, life, love, eternality, immortality, the grace and the benediction of God.

When my mind is imbued with spiritual truth, it is a law of elimination to all discords, all inharmonies, all injustices, all sins, all diseases, all false appetites.

I of my own self am nothing. But "I and my Father are one,"[3] and He that is within me is greater than any error that exists in the world. As I fill my consciousness with truth, love, and spiritual wisdom, I am a law of harmony, healing, and peace unto all who enter my spiritual household. "I can of mine own self do nothing,"[4] but since I and the Father are one, all that the Father has is mine: all the dominion, all the healing presence, all the forgiving power.

When my mind is filled with truth and love, I do not condemn. All who come to the meeting are forgiven, forgiven their sins of omission or commission. They come into His grace because my mind is filled with His grace, with His word, and with His truth. All who enter, enter the divine Presence and receive forgiveness and regeneration. They even find that the lost years of the locusts are restored to them by the divine Grace which God has given me.

Every word of truth which constitutes my consciousness is bread, wine, water, meat, life, and resurrection unto all who enter that consciousness.

You are not an isolated person separate and apart from every other person in the meeting. Each one is in you, and you are in each one, and all are in God. Those who come to this room to be a part of your consciousness of truth are all embodied in God, all one. There are not two, three, five, or six, as there seem to be. There is only one, all one in God-consciousness, all partaking of the divine name and nature.

ORDINATION BY GOD

The truth embodied in your consciousness is the healing art, the forgiving authority, the redeeming power. Without this truth in your consciousness, you are nothing. Even if you could be ordained by a legalized institution, you could not heal or bless anyone unless behind the authorization were your developed consciousness.

"If I bear witness of myself, my witness is not true."[5] *But since I and the Father are one, I am endowed with dominion from on High. "The Spirit of the Lord is upon me,"*[6] *and I am ordained to heal the sick, ordained by the grace of God, by virtue of the word of God which is now embodied in my consciousness.*

You who have been studying The Infinite Way or any other truly spiritual teaching one, two, five, or ten years must have a mind filled with truth, not memorized statements of truth. The substance of truth must have taken root within your consciousness. This makes you an authorized, ordained healer, forgiver, redeemer, one who sets others free from material sense. But you function in this way only when you recognize that it is not because you are *you* that you are become so mighty, but because you have become filled with spiritual truth, with the word of God which sets you free, and which sets all those free who come within range of your consciousness.

Now you will begin to see yourself in a new light. You will realize that you have spent these years filling your mind and soul with God's word, and that word of God has come to fruition, and all who reach and touch you are blessed and receive benediction.

YOUR NEWBORN CONSCIOUSNESS IS A BENEDICTION TO ALL WHO TOUCH IT

Realize that all those who come to a meeting are not coming merely to hear a person. They are entering the temple of God, which is your consciousness when it is filled with truth. The years of your study should have emptied out your old state of consciousness and built a new one made up of the word of God. This word of God which constitutes your newborn consciousness is life and truth and love to all who enter.

You do not direct your thoughts to those who come. They enter your consciousness and partake of whatever is its nature. If your mind or consciousness is full of sin and false appetites and false desires, they will enter there and feel it, be disturbed, and not at rest. But through your years of dedication you have no such consciousness any more. Furthermore, you know that whatever remains of human consciousness in you is not a power because only that is power which is given to you by the grace of God.

You will remember that all who enter that consciousness enter the spiritual realm of freedom and harmony. You are inviting into that spiritual household the guest of God, those who are ready to enter the spiritual realm. When they come, do not let them find your house empty. Do not let them find your consciousness devoid of truth and love. Be sure it is filled.

This not only is a prayer or meditation that will benefit all who are gathered in that place, but because you exist in consciousness, not in body or place, everyone, anywhere, who is reaching out for God-realization, is right where you are, receiving the benefit of God's presence. He may not and need not be a truth-student. He might be someone on the road in trouble, someone in the air, or someone reaching out for the realization or the help of God. Anyone reaching out to attain the presence of God is automatically where you are because you are the presence of God in expression—but only for one reason: your consciousness is unconditioned; it is not seeking any object.

You are not meeting together to seek money, fame, or anything that can be objectified. You are seeking only one thing: God-attainment; spiritual realization. Therefore, you present to this world pure consciousness, and pure consciousness is God. Because God is omnipresent, everyone reaching for God is where you are and is benefiting by this realization of the Presence.

When you enter a room dedicated to a spiritual purpose, there is quiet; there is stillness and confidence, and certainly there is an absence of hate, bigotry, bias, or jealousy. How did this peace get there? How were bias, bigotry, and hatred eliminated? The answer is clear. Those who entered that room brought the peace that is there. They did not find it there; there was no peace in the air, on the ceiling, or on the walls. Whatever peace, quiet, and confidence are in a room, whatever love is in a room, are brought there by those who carry those qualities in their consciousness. The reason that there is no hatred, jealousy, or discord is because it was not brought into the room.

It is a question of what you have in your house. What do you have in your consciousness? What do you bring into that room or building? It is the temple of God, but what makes it so? Not a ceiling, not walls, not a floor, not the beautiful surroundings. What makes it a temple of God? Your being there in peace, your being there in love, your being there in mutuality. It is not the building that is a temple of God: it is you who are the temple of God, if you leave human limitation, anger, fear, and jealousy outside and if you bring love and peace into the room through your

99

consciousness. How much you bring with you depends upon how much truth you know about what constitutes your consciousness, who you are, and what your true identity is.

CARRYING THE CHRIST-PEACE WITH YOU

Let us say that you have ten minutes, ten minutes to shut out the world, ten minutes away from the telephone, ten minutes for contemplating God and the things of God, ten minutes for spiritual realization. Remember, the world outside does not have the capacity to give ten minutes to this. It is only those who have in some measure been touched by the Spirit of God who have the capacity to sit for ten minutes in this contemplation:

What have I in my house? I have the full measure of Christ-peace. I have all that the Father has, for the Father has given His allness unto me. God has even breathed into me His life; therefore, I have in my consciousness life eternal. I, the Christ, am come that I might have life and that I might have it abundantly. I have in my house, in my consciousness, life, and life abundant, infinite life, eternal life.

I have an infinity of supply, because the Christ reveals that my heavenly Father knows that I have need of all these things, and that it is His good pleasure to give me the kingdom. I have the kingdom of God within me, and this is the Kingdom of all that I shall ever need. I have in my consciousness eternal life, infinite supply, divine peace.

As you contemplate this for five or ten minutes each day, you carry into your world the awareness of all that God is and all that God has as a gift that has been bestowed upon you by the grace of God. If you have contemplated that, you have brought the peace that passes understanding into the room.

100

Through your morning contemplation of truth, you make your home a temple of God. You do not find love in your home: it is not on the floor; it is not in the air; it is not on the ceiling. Love is not anywhere except where you bring it.

If the members of your family are to find love, they will find it because you, who are attuned to God, bring it there; and if they do not find love in your home, you have neglected to bring it there. You who have been led to a spiritual teaching have been given the Grace to know this truth, whereas those of your family or your business cannot bring peace to their homes or to their business. What you bring or what you find in your home or in your business, what you find in the world is what you bring to it. What have you in your consciousness?

I have the grace of God. I have the peace of God; I have been given quietness, confidence, and stillness. I have God's life, which is eternal, immortal life. I bring to my home, to my family, and to my business, that mind "which was also in Christ Jesus."[7] Knowing that I have all that God has, having no human desires and seeking nothing of any man except the privilege of sharing God's grace, makes my mind that mind that was in Christ Jesus. I already have all, therefore I pray only for the opportunity to share that which the Father has given me.

One of the reasons there is so much peace in any sanctuary is that people do not go there to get anything from anyone. They go only to spend an hour tabernacling with the Spirit of God and to share spiritual Grace. There is no peace when a person seeks to get something. The peace deepens if we are all conscious of being in a place to give and to share of this spiritual Grace, that each may contribute one to another the spiritual peace and comfort that God has given us in our period of meditation.

Keeping Your Temple Pure

Some organizations of long ago, and a few that I know about today, have a particular room which everyone in the group knows about. Each day at a certain hour, these people close their eyes and feel themselves in the actual room itself. Why this particular room? Because this room is kept pure; no one may enter it except in unselfish devotion; no one may enter it for any other purpose than for God-realization. Only those who are actively engaged in that particular work go there occasionally, so you can understand that those who reach toward it reach that purified consciousness that has no object and no purpose other than benediction.

As you maintain your consciousness on the level of spiritual unselfedness, living your life in a constant prayerful attitude of being a blessing and a benediction, not permitting any selfishness or any evil to enter it, your consciousness will be as pure as what we call heaven, and anyone reaching to your consciousness will receive healing, blessing, and benediction. Your consciousness is the temple of God, but it can be soiled by selfishness and self-interest, unless it is maintained pure in the light of truth.

You have to live in a constant attitude of no condemnation, leaving it to every person whether or not he wants to sin and be punished. What he does is not your affair. Your concern is to live always in an attitude of forgiveness. While maintaining this attitude of forgiveness, you do not walk around foolishly saying in the face of misconduct, "You are God's perfect child," but you do say that insofar as you are concerned, his sins are forgiven him.

My prayer is that you find God's grace. Whoever you are, whatever your crime, my prayer is that you find "the peace of God, which passeth all understanding,"[8] *that your consciousness be purified, so*

102

that even "though your sins be as scarlet, they shall be as white as snow"[9] in this moment of awakening.

While you recognize human evil and make continuous efforts to eradicate it, you must keep the temple of God which you are clean, and you do that by not bearing false witness. You may not yet have completely overcome your humanhood. This does not soil the temple which you are, however, because it is the motive that counts. You may not in one instant find full purification, but you are living by your motives, and your motives constitute the life you lead.

For a long, long time, you may not attain that complete purity where you can say, "I know that my consciousness is the temple of God because it is completely empty of self: self-desire, self-gain, self-will." But you can maintain it for periods of three, four, or five minutes, and you can do that as many times a day as you are willing to do it. You can set yourself apart and realize:

My consciousness now is the temple of God. All self-interest and self-desire are absent from this temple. I am here only as a transparency for the Spirit of God; I am here only that all in the world who are seeking light may find entrance to my consciousness and be illumined. I am here for only one purpose, that the sick reaching out for wholeness, the sinner reaching out for forgiveness, the dying reaching out for life, may find entrance into this tabernacle which I am and from which all sense of self is absent, so that the benediction which is the grace of God may touch all who enter here.

In that emptiness the world finds its entrance into your consciousness, and world-consciousness is dissolved. In the end the Master said, "I have overcome the world."[10] Why? Because that *I* was pure.

Purity does not consist of mere morality or honesty. That is not purity. Purity is an absence of self. The purity which is spiritual is an absence of personal desire and personal ambition. As you enter the tabernacle of God, have no hope, have no desire; in fact, do not even be there. Let your consciousness be as devoid of you as it can be. Let it be an emptiness; let it be a holy tabernacle; let it be an ark of the covenant; let it have no person. Then you can realize:

My consciousness is the temple of God. My consciousness is a house of refuge. Even the sinner can enter here and be forgiven. Let the sinner find peace; let the thirsty find drink; let the hungry find meat; let the sick find health; let the dead find life in this sanctuary which I am, this holy temple where I am not, but I AM.

On the spiritual path you must "die" to mortality. Once you have learned that there is no far-off God to whom you must sacrifice, to whom you must tithe, to whom you must give, you will know that your tithing, your giving, or your sharing is not for God. It is your mode of expressing gratitude for God's gift and God's grace to you. Your giving must have in it no seeking of a return. There is no giving of 10 percent to get 90 percent.

Watch this! You are a child of God only as your life is an expression of good without a single trace of desire for a return. On the human plane, when you do good for anyone, you look to him for good in return. You do not always get it. Your giving should be from the standpoint that it is God giving through you. It is God sharing through you. God asks no return. So it is that what you do, you do. Then there is no personal self, seeking a reward.

CAN A ROOM BECOME A TEMPLE OF GOD?

The Master taught us to pray in secret and to give our benevolences in secret. Why? There must be no selfhood around to claim credit; there must be no selfhood around to claim praise; there must be no selfhood around to receive thanks. True, the other person, for the sake of his salvation, must express gratitude and thanks, and give recognition and acknowledgment, but not for your sake. In the same way, you must express joy, peace, gratitude, and sharing, not for the other person, but only as a mode and means of letting God flow through you.

Can a room become a temple of God? No! Only *I* can be a temple of God; only Consciousness can be a temple of God; and you make the room holy by being there in an attitude of emptiness, a vacuum in the inner sanctuary or temple which *I AM.* Then, just as the Master's robe took on spiritual qualities and became the means whereby the woman who passed through the throng and touched the robe was healed, so can people enter a room where a dedicated consciousness has been praying, even after the person has left, and find healing, comfort, and forgiveness just as they might find it if they entered an empty church where there was a minister, a priest, or a rabbi of truly spiritual stature. A church that is graced by such a minister, priest, or rabbi becomes a sanctuary where a person may enter and find peace, healing, or supply. Anything can happen because the very room takes on the atmosphere of the consciousness of those responsible for it.

Anyone who is seeking the grace of God may reach that temple which you are and find peace because you have no condemnation, no criticism, and no censure within your consciousness. You are living as the Master lived.

"Come unto me, all ye that labour and are heavy laden, and I will give you rest."[11] *Drop your burdens. Here there is sanctuary; here you will find no criticism, no judgment. Here you will find forgiveness.*

105

Father, be a light unto those who enter this temple. Be their joy. Be their renewal. Come, all ye that labour, and all ye that are heavy laden. I, the Spirit of God within me, give you rest, security, safety, peace, and joy, and more than all else, I am come that you may have life, and that you may have life more abundant. This I, the Spirit of God in me, is here for the one purpose that you who look unto me might find this life. "My peace I give unto you: not as the world giveth, give I unto you."[12]

· 10 ·

The Widening Circle
of Prayer

MANY OF THE PROBLEMS the world faces are humanly insoluble, problems of such magnitude that they are beyond the mind or brain even of those who seek the highest offices in the nations of the world. This is a time that shakes man's faith. This is a time when people begin to think and fear and doubt. Yet this is our great opportunity. Why? Do we have a solution to these problems? Not any human solution.

The Master did not have a human solution to offer in his day. And yet he did have a solution for every problem of human experience. He taught recourse to an inner kingdom, an inner power that makes men free.

A person who has had some of the fruitage of the spiritual life will never forsake it. He may go through trials and tribulations, but he knows that he goes through these with a Presence that ultimately leads him into spiritual light and harmony. We must never forget that each one of us suffers in some measure as the world suffers. We cannot live completely unto ourselves and say that the suffering of mankind does not touch us. That would be impossible.

Those of us who are on the spiritual path have a bond with one another that makes our interest a common and united one. Our real life is lived in the withinness of our being, and we draw upon that withinness for supply, companionship, and outer relationships. Our interest is in bringing forth spiritual power, not only for ourselves or our families, but for the entire world.

We have the opportunity to live a life so spiritually governed that we will bear fruit richly and the discords of the world will not come nigh our dwelling place. That opportunity comes only through surmounting our problem, and that problem is the ability to rise above the use of the world's weapons, to rise above thinking in terms of human solutions, depending upon them, or believing that in any way they will ultimately solve the world's problems.

We render unto Caesar the things that are Caesar's. We pray for guidance as to whom to vote for. We go to the polls on election day and find no excuse to stay home. That is an obligation of citizenship. But we cannot expect that the world's problems will be solved that way. The world's problems will be solved spiritually. They will be solved without taking up the sword, without rebellion, without revolution, without taking sides. Certainly, as citizens, we vote for whoever it is that is revealed to us as representing the highest human form of government. But we should not put the responsibility upon any elected official to save the world.

Even though we may be living in a sense of greater security and peace than the world at large, nevertheless, we do owe a debt to the world, and, therefore, we take upon ourselves some of the responsibilities, the trials, and the tribulations of the world. Furthermore, when we go through some of the troubles of the world and bring to them our spiritual realization, we are contributing something to the overcoming of those troubles.

The important point is that the grace of God is not given to any individual for himself. There is no such thing as God giving His grace to a person for his own benefit, any more than that the sun shines exclusively for the Jones family, the Browns, or the Smiths.

God could no more give any one of us a blessing than God could give apples to one branch of a tree. The tree is a whole tree, important in the scheme of God. Therefore, apples must appear on all the branches of the apple tree. Roses must appear on every branch of the rosebush. How foolish it would be to pray for roses to be on one branch of one bush, or for apples to be on one branch of one tree! How foolish such a prayer would be in the sight of God!

How must it seem to God for us to pray, "Bless Mrs. Jones." Why Mrs. Jones? Why any more Mrs. Jones than Mrs. Brown or Mrs. Smith? "God bless our country." Why our country more than any other country on the globe? How is it possible for God to bless one and withhold from another? How would it be possible for the sun to shine in my garden and miss yours?

Scripture reveals that God's grace falls on the unjust as well as the just. How sinful it is to believe that God's grace flows only to good people! God's grace is meant not only for good people, but even more for the bad ones. Are we not told that the healthy ones need not a physician? Our prayer must be universal and include this wisdom:

God has no illegitimate offspring. The grace of God is meant for all the children of God. All God's grace is given universally to all mankind; and when an individual receives this Grace, it is not for himself but for the benefit of the world.

Why, then, do we not all receive the blessings of God equally? Those of us who in any degree find a lack or limitation of God's goodness find it only because we ourselves set up the barrier. We

109

are holding some people in condemnation, some races or some creeds, as if there were any race or creed in God. We have not only racial and national biases and bigotries but, stupidly enough, we have religious ones, as if God had any church. There is no church in God. There is no religion in God. God's relationship is not with edifices or man-made institutions. God's relationship is with Himself appearing as man, an indissoluble relationship.

With every advance in spiritual understanding that has come to us, we have placed our spiritual knowlege and attainment not only at the doorstep of our family, our neighbors, and our friends, but we have offered whatever of spiritual understanding or power we have been given to anyone within range of our consciousness who seemed to have a need. As we advanced still further in spiritual awareness, we began to pray for our community, nation, and world. Those who have been the longest on the path are giving some part of every day to prayer on world conditions.

In What Spirit Are We Praying?

World conditions will not lessen because some nation raises up a few more soldiers or a few more billion dollars to spend on armaments. Raising up armies does not lessen tension. If anything, it increases it. Tension is relaxed only through a spiritual activity. Men in all parts of the world are praying to this end, some along mystical lines and some along more orthodox lines. It is not the manner of prayer, however, that is a determining influence in life. It is the motive.

We may pray the highest kind of spiritual prayer, but if in our heart there is not the desire to see harmony, peace, and spirituality realized, our prayer is worthless. On the other hand, we could pray the most orthodox prayer that has ever been prayed, we could pray even as the pagans did. If in our heart is a desire for peace—I do

110

not mean victory; I do not mean a desire to get your way or my way, your country's way or my country's way—I mean that if there is a sincere desire to see the reign of the Christ on earth, the form of our prayer would make no difference because there is no God listening to the human voice. There is no God listening to Catholic prayers, Protestant prayers, or Jewish prayers. The God that answers prayer is Spirit, and It answers prayer according to the spirit of those who are praying.

In what spirit are we praying? Are we praying that the grace of God be made manifest among our friends and among our enemies? Are we praying that the innocent be lifted up and the guilty be healed? Then we are praying aright, and the form of our prayer is of no importance.

To many the prayer of petition is as outmoded as is the prayer of affirmation. But either of these prayers would be equally effective if in the heart of the person praying the motive were pure. No one can come to the throne of God except with a pure heart. To be pure in heart means to desire good, not only good for us, for our families, our nation, or our allies, but for friend and foe, white and black, Jew and Gentile. Until the heart is purified by the desire to see God's kingdom on earth, the prayer is of no avail.

THE EMPTINESS OF LIFE LIVED SOLELY ON THE HUMAN LEVEL

We who have witnessed the power of prayer in our individual experience and have begun to share it with our relatives, neighbors, and community know the richness that enters life through what we pour out from within us. The great masses of mankind know absolutely nothing about the peace that can be found through prayer. They know nothing of a spiritual union among people that makes them love one another regardless of differences of race or religion or of barriers created by borders. They know

111

nothing of the fatherhood of God and the brotherhood of man which unite us in one household of one family.

Their lives are drab, and they do not even suggest that there is any other kind of life. Their attention is focused in the thunder and lightning of the world, in the noises of the world, its troubles, excitements, and pleasures. If the masses could know something about the world of the Spirit, some of them at least would begin to open their eyes and desire what we who have learned about a life of prayer have discovered.

Yet there are thousands, probably millions, of persons in all parts of the world, longing inwardly to know something about the way of life by prayer. There is only one way to help them. It is not a human way. We cannot go searching up and down the highways and byways of the world asking, "Would you like to know about prayer? Would you like to find peace spiritually?" This we cannot do, but there is one thing we can do.

These persons who are seeking and have not yet found a way are responsive to prayer. If, in our daily meditations and prayers, we can remember the seekers and searchers, those who have not yet found their spiritual home and the kingdom of God within, and then realize that this God-love that is flowing through us is meeting their need, entering their consciousness and bringing awakening and light to them, we would be surprised at how rapidly many of them would be led somewhere to hear about a spiritual message. I am not speaking at this moment of waking people up to The Infinite Way. My interest goes far beyond that: it is in awakening mankind to the inner life, the life of prayer.

The mass of mankind has no place to go for its satisfactions, its profit or success, except to the outer world. As far as the persons who make up that mass are concerned, they have to fight their way through life, scheme, plot, or be lucky. They have no way to search

112

for peace except in the external realm. They have no way to search for a moment of quiet except by listening to noise. The outer noise stops the noise that is going on within them, and for a while at least they become unconscious of the turmoil within themselves. It is a way of life that is an escape.

INDIVIDUAL FOUNTAINS OF LIGHT

In our prayers, let our thoughts go out to the world. Let us embrace mankind in our consciousness, knowing that all those prepared for the Christ will meet the Christ, all those prepared for the grace of God will receive It. The prayers of those seeking to witness universal peace, universal harmony, universal health, and universal wealth will be answered, and they will be led to that spiritual fountain within.

Each one of us is a fountain of spiritual light bubbling over to be shared with any and everyone ready to experience it in proportion to his awareness of the truth that "the kingdom of God is within. . . ."[1] This must be released from within, first of all, by recognizing that we are a fountain of life and that we are willing to share this "water," this "meat," this resurrection, this life eternal, with all who are prepared to receive it. Then the next step is to go into the silence and there offer it to the world.

If we were to walk up and down the highways and byways telling this to the world, it would not be long before we would be ridiculed and persecuted, and the "pearl of great price"[2] that we have offered would be trampled upon. Wisdom teaches us not to give our spiritual riches to those who are not connoisseurs of spiritual things. This need not keep us from fulfilling our part because the promise of the Master is that if we pray in secret where no man knows that we are praying, if we pray that the world come to this

113

fountain of spiritual water and find the inner Kingdom, our prayer will reach those ready, receptive, and responsive to receive the benefit of that prayer.

All that we know secretly, silently, and sacredly within ourselves is answered openly and outwardly, but it is not the words or the thoughts in prayer that carry the power. The power is the motive. If there is a personal or selfish reason, it never will reach the throne of God and never will be answered. When our motive is that God's grace be made known, that God's presence be felt, that God's power be manifest to friend and foe in all lands, then our prayer is with power.

How shall we pray for the enemy? Shall we pray that he be successful in overcoming us? Is that possible for us, or is that a degree of unselfishness we have not yet attained? Our prayer, however, can and should be, "Father, open his eyes that he may see. Open his ears that he may hear." In doing this, let us not think for a moment that the only enemies we have are in faraway places. We have a few blind and deaf men right on this continent. Some of our enemies are in our own midst in very high places, not that they are evil—I would not even suggest such a thing—only that they are blind and deaf to the spiritual urge.

Suppose that you and I had a difference. You are on that side of the table, and I am on this side of the table. You are insisting that you are going to have your way, and I am insisting that I am going to have my way. Now, tell me, when do you think peace could come between us? Is there any hope whatsoever as long as you insist that you must have your way and I insist that I must have my way? No, that could go on to the end of time.

So it is in this present world situation. As long as the countries of the world are lined up on opposite sides of the table, there will be no peace. There may be an absence of a shooting war, but the peace will come only when the two present-day great powers sit on the same side of the table and say, "Let us work out the problems of the world." Then they will be worked out. No other way! You and I cannot do it individually on any other basis, and neither could we if we were in the White House or in the Kremlin.

The time is past in human history for victories. Laughingly, I say to you that the Allies were victors over Germany in World War I; laughingly, I say this to you, knowing what a mockery that victory was. Just as laughingly I say to you we defeated Germany and Japan in World War II. It is a mockery to believe that we were victors! Both of those victories were hollow things, and God forbid that we should win another victory like them! We cannot afford another such victory.

When we pray, we pray universally. We pray that all men's eyes be opened, that the kingdom of God be realized on earth as it is in heaven, that those who are in sin be lifted up and be forgiven —not punished. We never pray for anyone's punishment. Our prayer is that everyone be forgiven. We pray that those who are offending this world, who are against liberty, justice, and equality, be forgiven, that their eyes be opened, and then we will be contributing to the peace of the world far more than if we offered to carry a gun in the defense of peace.

Is it any different out in the world than it is with us in our homes? One of the difficult lessons on the spiritual path is to be able to look without resentment right at those who would rob, deprive, or persecute us, and pray, "Father, forgive them." Until we are able to look through the appearance and know its impersonal nature and nonpower, we are not even prepared for a spiritual ministry, and prayers from such a consciousness are wasted.

The Power of Pure Motive

Prayer, to be answered prayer, must come from a heart that is purged of personal and selfish motives, a heart that has for its desire that all men may know God's grace. This prayer silently spoken or thought not only sets the one who prays free but it sets mankind free. We can watch it in operation on the level of the family. We can use this silent, secret prayer in our household, confining ourselves to our immediate circle, and pray that God's grace be established. We embrace everyone in our consciousness until we have made peace with him and attained an absolute conviction that our desire is that the grace of God be his experience.

When we begin to see the fruitage in that small circle, then we are ready to lift our vision and go out into the community, to the seat of our government, to cross borders and look each nation in the face, each religion, and make peace: "Go thy way in peace. May God's grace be visited upon you. May you forever know the joy of living in His forgiveness and in His love, peace, and prosperity."

We can then go back to the altar, leave our gift, and pray:

Father, forgive me as I have forgiven those who have offended me. Father, may Thy grace be upon me as I have visited Thy grace upon them. I have prayed only that my sins be forgiven me as I have forgiven the sins of others. I pray only that Thy grace be upon me in proportion as I desire It to be upon those others.

All this is done silently, secretly, sacredly, and for one purpose: that God's grace be established on earth. Is there a better way of establishing God's kingdom on earth? Can we for a moment believe that the Christ-kingdom will ever come without love,

116

without forgiveness, without withdrawing condemnation and criticism? Is there anyone so much above judgment, criticism, or condemnation that he thinks God's grace should come to him and not to all mankind?

Among those who have realized even a tiny measure of God's grace, there is the realization: "I do not claim to have attained, not fully; but I am forgetting the sins which are past and am looking to the full demonstration of Christhood." If we recognize that for ourselves, we have to acknowledge that even if they have not yet attained their spiritual perfection, every man, woman, and child would like to forget their sins and open their souls to spiritual regeneration.

In this way harmony is established among us. Only when you know that the prayer in my heart is that God's grace be visited upon you, can you feel at peace with me. And I can feel at peace with you only when I know that you are looking in my direction, not with criticism, judgment, or condemnation for whatever human faults may still remain, but that you are looking toward me with no condemnation and with a "Father, forgive him. May Thy grace be established in him." That makes for the peace we feel in the presence of spiritual consciousness and that is responsible for the measure of peace among us.

WIDENING OUR VISION AND EMBRACING THE WORLD

Now we widen our circle and let our vision go beyond our immediate environment and look out at mankind with the same feeling that we have for one another. That same motive toward the world will bring the world into the circle of Christhood.

When individuals have differences and go to court or when nations quarrel and go to war, does not each one feel that he is right and that his cause is just? Are we a judge of whether this is

117

true or not? Are we able to judge who is right and who is wrong? Whether it is a fistfight, a lawsuit, or an international war, as long as we sit in judgment, the warfare will continue. All this will end when the judgment ends and when we are able to say, "I may have erred. The other side may have erred, but with God's grace, there will be no more erring, no more mistakes. There will be peace on earth as there is in heaven. There will be peace in my heart. There will be peace in your heart." This peace extends as we extend our vision and let our prayers encompass mankind.

Since the world does not know how to find its way to the Christ, someone must pray, and those prayers will be the light that will lead every seeker and searcher to one of the spiritual paths that bless.

Man's only defense against the evils of the world lies in prayer, but that prayer must be an open heart of love invoking divine blessing on mankind—not on us, on our race, on our creed, or on our nation, but on mankind. We begin this practice in our home, widening the circle to include our friends and more distant relatives. As we begin to witness the fruitage of what we are doing, we reach further until we are including all mankind in our prayer.

This explains what happens when someone wakes up in the morning and for no reason at all is led to turn on a radio or television program and finds a spiritual message being broadcast at that moment. Someone else may board a bus and find a pamphlet left on the seat which calls his attention to prayer. In one way or another, persons all over the world are being led to the spiritual life.

We have seen this principle in operation in The Infinite Way where no public means have been used to bring anyone to this message—no advertising, no proselyting—just prayer, the prayer that opens consciousness with no condemnation and invites the

118

world to find spiritual peace in prayer and meditation. It does not invite them to The Infinite Way: it merely says, "Open your hearts and souls to the reign of the Christ, to the realization of spiritual harmony, to the 'meat' that we have found within us. Open the eyes of this world to the springs of living waters within."

These prayers are unselfed prayers, and they bring fruitage after their own kind. Everyone knows the blessing he feels within himself when he does a good turn for someone unselfishly and impersonally. But what happens within us as we realize that people all over the world are being set free in the Christ, set free from problems, worries, and fears, set free to realize their spiritual identity through our prayers?

We need never be concerned that we will not know the fruitage of our prayers. In many different ways, it will be brought home to us. We will see the evidence of that Force and Power which we have been instrumental in loosing into the world. Release God into the world, but let us be sure we are not directing God to some friend's corner. Loose God. Release Him into this world that He may bless and redeem. In saving the world, we know that we are saved individually, for if this world goes, we go with it. There is no such thing as some who will be saved and some who will be lost—I am speaking now of a world cataclysm—if the terrors that every nation has in its store of armaments are loosed. There will be no saved and no lost: there will just be the dead and the dying.

The spiritual students of the world have within their power the ability to change the world in this century into a heaven on earth. How? By prayer and meditation, by letting loose this "bread" that they have stored up within them.

To pray spiritually really means to have a feeling that our arms are outstretched, even when they are not physically outstretched, and that we have all the world in our arms and are saying, "Father, forgive them their sins. Father, open their eyes and their ears. Father, I pray that Thy love may shine upon them, that Thy grace may feed and sustain them."

This is prayer, when the arms are outstretched and the whole world is inside: the world of friends, relatives, and enemies. All the world is inside, and we are saying, "God's love is upon us; God's grace is within us; God's benevolence shines in our hearts." This altitude of prayer brings forth a spiritual response within us and the accompanying spiritual fruitage.

· 11 ·

Individuality
Revealed Through Prayer

THE PURPOSE OF PRAYER is to bring the Spirit to our individual experience, so that this parenthesis* may be permeated with the Spirit and the fourth-dimensional substance called the Christ may come into activity. This is a transcendental Presence, a Substance, Essence, Activity, or Reality which can never be seen, heard, tasted, touched, or smelled. It is so real that It can whisper in our ear, "Do not drive up this street: drive up that one." It can prevent us from making an investment or lead us to a bookshelf where we might find the one book that can meet our need for us at a particular time. It can even go before us so that our banker makes the loan that he refused to make the day before.

It is an unseen spiritual Influence, and the person who is illumined has contact with Its essence. Two words for illumination used in the Orient are "sattori" and "darshan." Christian mysticism has a word for us, too, a beautiful word: Grace. "My grace is sufficient for thee,"[1] "My" meaning the invisible spiritual Center or Source. We live by Grace; we can do all things through the grace of God.

*See the author's *A Parenthesis in Eternity* (New York: Harper & Row, 1963).

The transcendental Presence must become a living experience, permeating our consciousness, flowing through us to the extent that the fingers tingle with It, and the toes. It is a reality, even though the human mind cannot understand It, the human eyes cannot see It, and the human ears cannot hear It. It is so real that when It happens we know It, and there are no questions. When anyone asks the question, "How may I know if this is real?" he has not yet experienced It. When a person does, It is unmistakable, not only in Its manner of expression, but in the fruitage. When a person is touched by the transcendental Presence, something in his life will be better: his health, supply, morals, home, family relationships, or business. The more he contacts It, the more his life will be an outer expression of an inner Divinity.

CREATION UNFOLDING

This experience will never be fully attained until through prayer and meditation the veil of illusion that separates us from reality is rent. Let us imagine that we have before us a block of clay. Out of the clay, human forms are molded, but in that molding, the forms do not lose their contact with the clay. They are clay itself, formed.

So in creation, God is the Father, the Substance, and men and women the children: God, the Father; God, the children. But the children are still of God. They are made of the basic Substance, formed in Its image and likeness. The Father constitutes the substance of the son, as clay constitutes the substance of the molded forms.

God is an invisible substance, and therefore, the child of God is also invisible. We cannot see, hear, taste, touch, or smell the child of God. He is just as much Spirit as God is Spirit and is formed of the same substance as God, which is incorporeal Spirit.

So we have God, infinite perfection, and we have His sons and daughters, also infinitely perfect. Made in the image and likeness of God, they are as perfect as their Source. At this stage, men and women need no prayers. They have nothing but divine qualities. They lack nothing; so they do not have to get back to anything. They have no needs. They are living in the truth: "Son, thou art ever with me, and all that I have is thine."[2]

We begin to understand creation as the word Consciousness or the word *I* takes on new meaning. "In the beginning God,"[3] but since using the word God indicates something separate and apart from our Self, let us begin with the truth that *I*, Consciousness, am God. Consciousness is God, but all I am is consciousness; therefore, I am the divine Consciousness in expression.

There cannot be an unexpressed Consciousness. That would be unconsciousness. Consciousness must be Consciousness expressed, Consciousness manifested, or *I* expressed, *I* manifested. Let us call whatever that Consciousness is as manifestation, man, or to go further, let us call It individual being: *I*, God, manifest as I, the son. That Consciousness is inseparable and indivisible from Its self:

I, the son, am forever in and of I, *the Father, for we are one.* I, *God, being infinite, nothing can exist outside of that infinity. Therefore,* I, *the Father, exist in and as I, the son, and the son in the Father.*

In this light we see that the qualities of God are manifest as the qualities of the son. The qualities of infinite Consciousness are the qualities of individual consciousness, because only the one Consciousness forms Itself as individual you and me. Since we are formed of Consciousness, the essence, substance, and activity of our being is the essence, substance, and being of God, the *I*. All

123

we have to do is to keep that word *I* in mind and remember: All that *I*, divine Consciousness, have is yours as individual consciousness.

In this awareness, we do not live by might or by power. We live by *My* Spirit, by *My* Consciousness. The consciousness of the Father is the consciousness of the son. The life of the Father is the life of the son. The Soul of the Father is the soul of the son. We have a life lived as the gift of God because we are heirs of God, and all that God has is ours. We are formed of the substance of God, and this entire creation is spiritual: *I*, the Father, infinite divine Consciousness, manifest as individual consciousness, yet always one. This is the spiritual, perfect creation.

But something happened. A belief in two powers arose. We do not know how it was possible for it to arise or anything about it. We only know that the moment it did, the perfect man and woman lost their God-identity and were separate and apart from God.

If you and I knew that there is only one Power, none of us would have any problems to solve. We would have no evils to meet, no lack or limitation, no pain or old age. If there is only one Power, there could be nothing to interfere with the perfection of God's creation. It is because we have accepted in our consciousness the belief in two powers that we are trying to find the truth that will free us of this belief and restore us to the Father's consciousness.

Let us again imagine these clay figures symbolizing spiritual man. Now let us clothe them, until these spiritual men and women are entirely lost from sight, and all we see are suits and dresses. We do not know what is underneath. We have been looking at suits and dresses for so many generations that we think those suits and dresses constitute all there is to men and women.

We are not going to waste any time asking why it happened,

how it happened, or how it could happen. All we are going to do is accept the fact that one day we were born and we had no awareness of our original spiritual identity. We believed that we had two human parents, being unaware of the truth that there really is only one Parent, the divine Consciousness which we are and which we manifest as individual being. But we are told now that we are children and have human parents. It is not long before we discover that our life is controlled by everything and everybody in the world. We are ordered about by our parents, our aunts and uncles, our schoolteachers, then by employers, later on by the government, and finally by an income tax department.

All this time we have not been aware that we are imbued with God-given dominion over everything in the earth, in the heavens, and in the waters beneath. We are ignorant of our identity. We are ignorant of the fact that we are heirs to a tremendous fortune, to all the spiritual riches. We are ignorant of the truth that our life is God, so we protect our life and do all sorts of things to a life that is already infinite and cannot be changed.

We live in ignorance of the truth about our Creator and about ourselves: our nature, character, being, life, and body. Above all, we are in ignorance about our dominion. So we live in a little world of human creation, the world that our great-grandparents, grandparents, parents, and schoolteachers helped to create in their minds and pass on to us. They have us encased in a little world in which we are almost nonentities, struggling with three billion other people for a livelihood and with everybody in the world having jurisdiction over us.

We try our best to get along in the world—and I do not have to tell you that I have been in the same position in which you have been—not finding this world a very satisfactory place, not disliking it enough to try to get out of it, yet disliking it enough to resort

125

to all kinds of escapisms to avoid having to face the fact that we are nonentities struggling for survival against terrible odds and with almost no control over our own lives.

MAKING THE RETURN JOURNEY

In Scripture, this life that I have just described is termed the prodigal experience. We were born in a far country, far from our Father's house, completely unaware of our true identity, and with a personal self: I must fend for myself; I must protect myself; I must support myself; I, I, I, I, I, as if there really were an I separate and apart from the great *I* that I am. So here is this little I on a merry-go-round, traveling fast and going nowhere, and eventually realizing the unsatisfactoriness of that condition.

Many millions of persons go through an entire lifetime kicking against this kind of life and doing nothing about it, eventually passing on and having to come back and go through the same parade all over again. They do not even know that they are heirs, but having heard of God, the word begins to percolate in their thought, and most of them come to the place where they say, "Now, wait a minute, wait a minute! You talk about a God, but surely any God worth the name of God could not be responsible for the chaos on earth. Any God worthy of the name of God could not possibly tolerate my being in this condition." So they begin to puzzle about that word God. If they allow themselves to puzzle about it just a little while, a miracle sets in, and off they are on a search for God.

The human being has that divine Being hidden down inside in consciousness, so deep down that there is no awareness of Its being there. But someone receives an illumination that recognizes that underneath those suits and dresses there is the body of God, that original Spirit-body. Impossible, impossible! We go over and look

126

in the mirror, and It is not there. We search, but we cannot find It because It will never reveal Itself to us through our eyesight. Only spiritual insight will tell us that underneath these clothes there is a temple made by and of God. The creative Principle, God, formed it and formed it of the substance of Himself.

Since our mirror does not tell any story like that to us, the question is: How are we ever going to come into the knowledge and demonstration of our true being and body? How are we going to be able to penetrate beneath the surface so that we see something more than the eyes see and hear something more than the ears hear? The person who first caught such a spiritual glimpse had a transcendental vision within himself. It was an inner vision or an inner glimpse of reality that enabled him to see that we are not mortals, that we do not have bodies of flesh and blood: we are immortal and the body is the temple of God.

To all the five senses, we are mortals, born, aging, dying. We have limited lives, limited mentalities, limited strength. But to this limited sense a few men and women of intuition and vision say, "No, no! Know ye not that ye are the temple of God, and God dwells in you? Know ye not that ye are the image and likeness of God? Ye are spiritual! Ye are of the substance of God."

We, in our dullness, go back to that mirror again and say, "It cannot be; this is just human flesh, heir to all the ills and accidents of the world."

But again, these great spiritual men and women of all ages keep saying, "Do not believe what you see or hear. God, Truth, is not in the appearance. God is in the 'still small voice.'[4]"

We have been told about our true identity, our true Selfhood, but we have heard it only with the hearing of the ears. We have not yet discerned it, nor unlocked whatever it is that is blocking the entrance to our Self. While a person is walking around, working hard to earn a living, struggling with sin and disease, his real free and independent Self, the individualization of all that God is, is hidden inside his consciousness, probably rolled up like a ball, tight. The Orientals call it an "onion." They have discovered that this process of knowing the truth, of searching for God, is like taking the skin from the onion, one onion skin at a time. It does not seem to do much toward getting to the center; nevertheless, something has happened, even with the removal of one layer of onion skin.

As we imbibe truth through knowledge of, and devotion to, truth and through meditation, layer after layer of the outer false self drops away. When we finish removing every skin from the onion, we have nothing left. We have that Nothing which is All, that Nothing which is spiritual, that Nothing which is the essence of life. Scripture reminds us, "He . . . hangeth the earth upon nothing."[5] That is the very Nothing that we find in the center of the onion, and that is the very Nothing that we find when every bit of our humanhood is taken from us. When we have completely divested ourselves of self, there is Nothing left, and that Nothing is the *I* that we are.

Piercing the Veil

If we are wise, we will never call our humanhood the Christ, nor try to make our humanhood spiritual. There is, therefore, no reason to bemoan the fact that we are not humanly perfect while we are on this Path seeking our true identity. None of us can be humanly perfect. That is an impossibility! If we were, we might well fail in our journey. The moment a person is satisfied with himself, with his demonstration, supply, or companionship, he has lost the opportunity of attaining heaven. Only in dissatisfaction with humanhood, even when it is good, do we go higher. We quickly get away from unhappy and unhealthy humanhood, but

128

our journey is much slower when we try to rise above healthy or wealthy humanhood.

The person who is very righteous also has a hard time getting into heaven because the self-righteousness of human good bolsters the ego. Sometimes even metaphysical students who have attained health and supply boast about it as if they had accomplished Christhood Itself, instead of realizing that while all this good may be an indication of progress on the Way, it is not Christhood. Christhood is reached when we have gone beyond good human-hood, happy humanhood, righteous humanhood, or wealthy hu-manhood, pierced the veil and beheld our true identity.

What are we going to find when we reach our Christhood? Jesus called himself by the name of *I*, and he said, "I am come that they might have life, and that they might have it more abundantly."[6] This inner Self of us which is hidden inside that flesh, blood, and bones, our own Christhood, is always saying to us:

I *am come here within you to be your life everlasting.* I *am to resurrect you out of any tomb into which you may have fallen: the tomb of sin, the tomb of disease, the tomb of poverty, the tomb of unhappiness. Into whatever tomb you have fallen,* I, *your Christ-self, am here to resurrect you, to bring you back to the Father's house so that you will "die" to that flesh and blood and bone belief, and actually witness your Self as you are, the Christ, the perfect son of God, the perfect offspring of the perfect Substance, Life, and Being.*

In the beginning God sent Himself forth as our incorporeal, spiritual being. As His son, our name is Christ, but we identify ourselves by the name *I*.

God is the Self of me, and therefore, it is my Self that is omni-present, omnipotent, omniscient. It is not some self from thousands

129

of years ago. It is not some self that is up in heaven. It is my Self, thy Self, our Self, the one infinite, divine Self which is omnipresent, omniscient, omnipotent, the Self of me.

If I mount up to heaven, I have this Omnipotence, Omniscience, and Omnipresence with me, but if, temporarily or in belief, I walk through hell or "the valley of the shadow of death,"[7] I need only say, "I," and smile at the idea that I could ever have accepted a limited self that was born and will die, when there is only one Self, and that is the God-Self.

The outer self is the masquerade which is born of the belief in two powers, but I *am spiritual Being.*

I *am nothing that can be seen, heard, tasted, touched, or smelled.* I *am nothing that anyone can get his mind or his fingers on because* I *am nowhere between the toenails and the top of the head. No one can grasp* Me *because if he tries he will get his hands on nothing.* I, *Consciousness, Spirit, am nothing tangible, nothing physical, nothing mortal, nothing material, and in that nontangibility or incorporeality you have* Me *as* I *am, that* I AM *which* I *was in the beginning with God, incorporeal real Selfhood.*

The object of prayer is to strip this outer sense of self away until we get back into the withinness of our own being, and there find ourselves to be that *I.* This is the return to the Father's house, to be robed again in the royal robes of a prince, and given the royal ring of authority which is symbolic. It merely means that we have discarded our mortal skin for our spiritual identity, and now we can say, "Yes, I know that *I AM. I* am the embodiment of the power of resurrection and of life eternal. *I* am the embodiment of my food, clothing, housing, and transportation. *I* am the Way. My whole life now walks the way of *I.* I dedicate my life to this Way."

What are we doing while we are realizing all this? We are

praying. This is prayer. This is knowing the truth that makes us free. This is communion with our inner Self. This is meditation. We are contemplating the truth of our Self. Our eyes can be closed or open when we are doing this. We can do it lying in bed, but if we fall asleep, we will have to begin all over again when we wake up. There is no harm in falling asleep during meditation, but we should not make a practice of doing it every time or we will not get acquainted with the *I* that we are. Knowing the *I* comes, not with deadness or unconsciousness, but with spiritual alertness, with the ability to be vigorous but not forceful.

Prayer, then, is a recognition of our true identity. It is an acknowledgment of the infinity of our own being. At first, prayer has a great many words and thoughts because the whole idea is new. We have to rehearse it; we do not believe it; we even go over to the mirror to see if the body is changing and find that for a long while it is not. Now we know that hidden within us, indwelling, is the *I* that we are, and our given name is only a courtesy name. The real name is *I*, and the Self of one of us is the Self of every one of us.

When we realize that locked up inside of us is *I*, we will learn to meditate and pray. We will make that *I* talk to us before we get through with It. We will open out a way for that imprisoned *I* to get out and be the "still small voice" for which we are listening, and sometimes It will thunder in our ears, because now we know that this *I* that I am is locked up inside of us, just as the clay figure is locked up inside of that suit or dress. When we rip off the suit or dress, we see the clay figure. As we rip this outer mental selfhood away, we find *I* in the midst of us: *I* am here; *I* am there; and *I* am everywhere.

Let this glorious *I* shine forth because It is Spirit. It is God in action. It is God individualized. Let us open our consciousness and let this *I* shine forth.

· 12 ·

Living by Prayer

TO LIVE BY PRAYER means to reach a state of consciousness where we come into conscious oneness with the Presence, that inner Source, and live without taking thought, without struggle, and without striving. Prayer is undoubtedly the highest way of life there is. It was the way of the Master who not only lived by prayer, but often went away for forty days and forty nights of prayer.

Prayer can be a hymn of gratitude that the kingdom of God, all the Father has, was established within us from the beginning. Prayer can be a recognition of our relationship with God as heir of God and joint-heir to all the heavenly riches. Prayer can be the recognition of the spiritual nature of the child of God and the spiritual nature of creation.

One thing prayer must not be: it must not be a going to a God of Spirit and asking for something material. If prayer is to bear fruit, It must be a recognition of the omnipresence of spiritual good, but that does not mean expecting that prayer to be answered in terms of a new house or a new automobile.

A life of prayer is a continuous recognition of the spiritual nature of God, the child of God, and the universe of God. Prayer must be a recognition of the spiritual nature of all law as being of God, and therefore spiritual, good, and full of justice. This breaks any bondage to material, mental, medical, or legal laws.

Prayer is an attitude of listening. Prayer is a recognition that we do not live by anything in the material realm. Prayer is an awareness that God is not in the whirlwind, and by whirlwind we mean any of the physical manifestations of error or discord. God is not in sin, disease, or accidents: God is in the "still small voice."[1]

If we want to experience the presence of God, is there any other way of attaining it than by recognizing that we must hear the "still small voice"? When we hear It, we receive some spiritual awareness. It does not necessarily mean an audible message, but every time that we receive some inner impulsion from the spiritual Presence, the Voice has been uttered, and some phase of earthly discord melts.

Prayer can take the form of the recognition of God as the solution to every problem. Any time that we are aware of a problem of any nature, even on a national or international scale, let us remember that we can solve it by prayer. God is the only permanent solution, the only solution that can bring forth justice, equity, equality, or abundance. Living a life of prayer means living the life that recognizes God as the solution to every problem.

Rise Above the Level of the Problem

We cannot meet a problem spiritually on the level of the problem. We must turn away from the problem as it appears. The quickest way to do this is to go within to the realization that this is a spiritual universe and, therefore, there must be a spiritual solution even to what appears as a physical condition, a financial situation, or a business problem.

Often when the problem concerns money, the first instinct is to get on a mental merry-go-round, worrying about how the money is going to come, where it is going to come from, and thinking of the possibility of its not coming. If we are living by prayer, our attitude is that the solution to this is God, not so many dollars. This immediately takes us out of "this world"² and lifts us into "My kingdom."² This is a spiritual universe, and there must be a spiritual answer.

It will not be easy to receive an answer from within if we are seeking a physical or material answer because the spiritual universe does not speak to us in material language. We must be able to translate the appearance, so that even if the problem is something as concrete as money, business, or a relationship, we turn within to recognize the spiritual nature of the universe. The very moment that we translate this universe into Spirit, we are praying aright.

This is a spiritual universe. I know, God, that when I hear Your voice, the earth will melt: the sense of physicality will dissolve, this material sense. When I hear Your voice, when I feel the assurance of Your presence, the material, finite, limited sense of existence will disappear, and I will have a spiritual answer and a spiritual kingdom.

Prayer Brings the Awareness of a Presence Within

Some complain that this is not absolute enough, that it is duality. I plead guilty to that. I have not risen so high myself that I have done away with God, nor have I done away with myself, so there still seems to me to be a "me" and God. But I have no hesitancy in going within in communion. As a matter of fact, I am on such terms with God that sometimes I can have a little quarrel with Him. Once in a while I turn within and say, "God, You had better listen to me, or I am going to go off somewhere and leave You alone, and You will miss me." He seems to understand, and then I get a smile inside and say, "All right, we have

134

made up. We are back again. But You were neglecting me!"

There are some who find fault with that, too, but there is that inner communion, that inner feeling of a Presence. I know right well that I would not be on earth if there had not been God to express as me. I know that I could never be on a spiritual path if Something greater than myself had not directed me and kept my feet on the Path when other temptations came. So I have no hesitancy in recognizing that there is a God-presence, and if sometimes I seem to be missing the mark in some way, I turn within and say, "You know, You put me here. Now do not go back on me!"

There have been times during classes when I have felt that there was nothing left to say, and I have had to turn within: "Well, Father, now You know something has to be said. You have to do the saying." Somehow or other, it comes, but I definitely know why. I know that I am an instrument. I know that those who are in class are instruments. They are not there because they humanly want to be there. Something greater than the human personality keeps a person on the spiritual path when there seems to be no fruitage or when there seems to be no answer from the Father. Yet he cannot leave the Path. Perhaps it is because the question comes up, "Where shall I go?" So he stays!

A Realization of Omnipresence, Omnipotence, and Omniscience Is Prayer

There are times when we wonder if, at the moment, we are under the jurisdiction of God, or if, in some way, we have strayed or become separated from God. In moments like that, and they come to everyone, a form of prayer is this recognition:

Whither shall I go from thy spirit? or whither shall I flee from thy presence?

135

If I ascend up into heaven, thou art there: if I make my bed in hell, behold, thou art there.

If I take the wings of the morning, and dwell in the uttermost parts of the sea;

Even there shall thy hand lead me, and thy right hand shall hold me.
—Psalm 139:7–10

The word "Omnipresence" comes, and we find ourselves right back in the kingdom of God. Omnipresence! To dwell in the realization of Omnipresence is a form of prayer. It is acknowledging the presence of God where we are: heaven or hell, death, whatever or wherever it may be.

It is acknowledging that there is only one Power, and that the appearance, however frightening its aspect, is not a power. Therefore, let it go on appearing. Since it is not a power, we do not try to get rid of it. We do not try to overcome it. We do not try to resist it. We acknowledge Omnipotence: "God is omnipotence. Omnipotence is within me, and there is no power external to me." We disregard the appearance, and our prayer, which is the recognition of Omnipotence, is answered.

Prayer is a recognition of the word "Omniscience." That is a reminder that we know not how to pray or what to pray for, because we do not know what is good for us. We think we know what we would like to have, but so does a child who is reaching out for a pound of chocolates, which do not always prove to be so good as they look. Our safest prayer is the word "Omniscience":

God is the all-knowing. I do not have to know anything; I do not have to make a decision. If I am holding open this line of commun-ion, I can wait to hear God's decision because God is omniscience. God knows whither I shall go, and why, and when. If I am holding open the inner line of prayer through listening, Omniscience will

136

reveal Its plan to me. The all-knowing Intelligence will disclose Its way, Its will, Its plan, Its direction, Its guidance, Its protection.

Since we carry our Christ within us, and Its name is Omniscience, why do we have to use words and thoughts? Why can we not just rest and let It perform Its works? That is what happens. We have an experience. It is like a movement or transition in consciousness, and we say, " 'Whereas I was blind, now I see.'[3] The Christ really is my identity. I have nothing to do but *let* the Christ live my life." Now we are at the place where we heal with a smile, because we are no longer dealing with corporeality in a mild form or a serious form. Now we are dealing with truth, and we are letting the truth make us free.

We must pray without ceasing. It may seem impossible to do this while we are living a human life, but I say it is possible. It is a matter of practice. It is a matter of dominion, a matter of determining to live by prayer, but knowing also what is meant by the listening attitude of prayer.

There are steps along the way of prayer, beginning with that preliminary step of practicing the presence of God, pondering or contemplating whatever it is that is within us of a spiritual nature. I cannot begin a meditation by saying, "I am God," because I am faced with all the mistakes of my humanhood, and I would be calling myself a liar. Rather than do that, I acknowledge that there is something of God about me or within me, that there is something to be attained, something to be known. So I ponder It, Its qualities, Its nature, and Its activity.

Eventually, through this kind of practice, we come to such an inner stillness that the outside world does not trouble us so greatly; we do not react to it so much, and it becomes less and less real to us. We begin to have less fear of the powers of this world, a greater reliance and confidence in the Infinite Invisible, and we are beginning to transfer our faith and our fears in the outer world to a conviction, an assurance, and an inner peace within ourselves.

We are still in duality because we have this divine *I* which we are and this human being out here who has not entirely found his way home. He is getting closer. The Father is coming out to meet him; the *I* is announcing Itself. The *I* within and the person without are getting better acquainted. I think they are beginning to love each other. There is a warmth, an attachment developing, a companionship, a communion. It is still duality. In fact, the whole ministry of Jesus Christ was duality, except in the brief revelation in which he disclosed his true identity.

If we abide in the Word and let the Word abide in us, if we begin to commune with the divine Spirit within us, get friendly with It, and reach a place where we really can have a feeling of oneness with It, the day comes when, in a deep meditation, we disappear completely. All trace of us is lost, and only *I* remain. We are looking out at this world, not as a human being, but as *I*, without physical form, absolutely incorporeal. We may be up in the sky looking down, or under the ocean looking up, because now we fill all space. Just as God fills all space, so does God manifest fill all space, and we are that Omniscience, Omnipotence, and Omnipresence while we are in the deepest part of our meditation. We have now found our way home.

At this point, the vast majority of those who have had the Experience return to the world and continue the life of duality. They live the life of human beings on earth, and at the same time they live the life of spiritual identity within themselves: they live in two worlds. Many do not recapture the secret of what has taken place, and they live very unhappy lives, because the Experience may never come again. They live wholly out here in their human-hood, never again returning to their spiritual estate.

138

THE MISSION OF THE MYSTIC

There are records of some who have attained the full illumination and left their bodies behind for burial, while they went on to live the balance of their experience in spiritual incorporeality. But most of the great mystics, and more especially those who have founded basic religions, have been content to live on earth as human beings, while inwardly living their spiritual life for the benefit of presenting their work and their teaching to the world, giving the world the benefit of their revelation.

Sometimes this is a voluntary act on the part of the particular mystic who feels it is more important to sacrifice himself to the life on earth for the greater good of others, and sometimes it is because the mystic is under orders from those spiritual lights who have left the corporeal scene. Behind this world there is a hierarchy of those who have attained their full illumination and who still influence those on earth who are spiritually attuned. So it is that sometimes under orders, the mystic remains on earth for the purpose of conveying his message. What message?

It is the message that there is a Father within. The closer we get to living with this Father, relying on Him, the more harmonious, joyous, and fruitful our outer life will be. The greatest revelation is given to those who are prepared for the sacrifice that is entailed, the sacrifice of what we might call prosperous human living, the sacrifice of the human good, so as to live in a dedication to service. In that revelation the duality disappears, and *I* reveals Itself as individual being, God incarnated as individual being. This is spiritual sonship, or Christhood.

In the case of Jesus, something further took place. The *I* that is God and that was manifested as *I*, the Christ, or son of God, permeated human consciousness, and Jesus could say, "He that seeth me seeth him that sent me.[4] . . . I am the way, the truth, and the life."[5] When he said that, his Jesushood was completely gone. The world saw his physical body, but he was looking out from the body of light and was totally unaware of all those around him. He was aware only of himself, speaking as God, as divine Christhood: "I am the way, the truth, and the life." We would say, "The *I* of me is the Christ. Christhood is my real identity." That is still acknowledging our personal sense of being, but Jesus had reached the place where there was no more Jesus-being. There was only the Father revealing Himself as the son.

The few great mystics who have attained that light, as the Master did, maintained it not continuously while on earth but only in periods of illumination. The rest of the time they lived 100 percent inwardly as the Christ, but they also recognized the limitations of their physical form and were content to tabernacle among us as physical form.

Such a high state of consciousness is attained step by step. First comes the recognition that, although to sense we are human beings, there is a divinity within us; then comes the attempt to return to our original state by tabernacling, communing, and acknowledging God until most of the human selfhood peels itself off, and we have transcended that stage of humanhood.

This I *that I am is my true Selfhood, and this that walks the earth is the finite sense of It, the mask, called* persona, *personality, human identity. At least I do now know that* I *in the midst of me is mighty. I know that* I *in the midst of me is the Christ, and I carry my own Christ wherever I go. That Christ is my meat, my wine, and my water. It is my supply. It is the cement of my human relationships. I do not have to look outside for any powers of good, and I do not have to fear any outside powers of evil, for I and the Christ of me are one, and this Christ of me is my divine Selfhood, my divine protection, my divine maintenance and sustenance.*

Prayer is a two-way channel: it is our going back to God, and then God coming forward to us. Yet the whole of it takes place within our consciousness, because we do not reach any God outside of us anywhere. We reach the kingdom of God within us. We can always pray because we can always blink our eyes and look inside ourselves.

Sometimes I look up into my forehead; sometimes I look down in the direction of my heart. I have no belief that God is entombed in my body anywhere. It is only that my attention must be directed somewhere, and so I am either looking up into the space behind my forehead or I am looking down toward the heart area just as a matter of centering my attention, but always with the same word, "Father! Speak, Father! Guide me; instruct me," or "What is Thy will? Thy will be done, not mine."

Often, when there are matters requiring a decision, I turn in the same way: "What is Thy will? Do not let me do this thing because I like to do it; do not let me do it because I want to do it; and do not let me refrain from doing it because I do not want to do it. Make Thy will clear. Thy will be done, not mine, and I really mean that I want to do Thy will, not mine. Only please make it clear."

We do not have to talk to God in any sanctimonious tone of voice as if He were some kind of holier-than-thou being. We talk to God the way we would talk to our father or mother, sister, brother, or anyone we love. If we love the Lord our God with all our heart, we can talk to God with a sense of humor, if we have one. The main thing is that we pray, and praying means making ourselves subject unto God, recognizing the omnipotence of that

141

He that is within us, and, therefore, certainly greater than any he that is in the world.

When we turn our attention within ourselves so that the voice of God may be heard, the will of God may be made evident, or the presence of God may become tangible, we are living by prayer. We create a vacuum within ourselves, so that we can be filled full by the Presence that is within us. This is prayer even if there are no words. If we turn within without a word, just with a listening attitude, we are praying because we have opened a way for the "still small voice" to reach us. Just to close our eyes and open our ears is one form of prayer. It is listening for the way of God to be made evident. All this is prayer, and it is communion.

Opening the Line to God Through a Listening Attitude

To live by prayer requires a recognition that God is not in the problem: God is in the silence. It means turning away from the problem within and, by developing the listening attitude, receiving the answer. We do not always receive an answer when we are praying, nor do we always receive an answer at the moment when we would like to receive it. But once we have prayed, once we have tuned in and listened, we can then go on about our business and be assured that the answer will come in its own good time. It may be when we are taking no thought at all about the problem. It may be when we are taking a bath, when we are about our housework, or when we are attending to business. But we can be assured that God will interrupt whatever we are doing, even waking us up out of sleep, to give us the necessary answer.

Our position is not one of presuming to dictate to God when the answer should come. Our function is to pray without ceasing. That means listening without ceasing, not keeping the mind so occupied with nonessentials that there is not room for that "still small voice" to creep in at any moment of the day or night. It is even wisdom, immediately on getting into bed, consciously to remember, "I am not going to sleep. I am going to rest, and while I am resting, my consciousness is open to God, whether awake or asleep." In my own experience, the result of that was that I was awakened in the middle of the night whenever it was necessary, and some of my most inspired revelations have come when I have had to jump out of bed to make notes. The important thing is never to go to sleep without praying and without keeping our line to God open.

Listening and keeping the lines of communication open is prayer—assuring ourselves of Omnipresence, of divine Grace, assuring ourselves over and over that this is a spiritual universe. Whatever form it takes, it is prayer! The only time the form is wrong is when we are telling God what we want, or when. Then we can be assured we are not praying: we are trying to be wiser than God. The answer to every problem comes when God utters His word. Then the earth melts, and the problem disappears.

Prayer Is the Means of God's Fulfillment As Us

Prayer must always be the means of communion between us and the Father within. It never has anything to do with a person, a thing, or a condition, and never concerns itself with a material manifestation. Prayer, to be prayer, must be kept on the spiritual level, recognizing that the solution to any problem will come through a message from God or through a directive from God.

It is through prayer that we are at-one with God and commune with Him. It is through prayer that we receive Grace through God or from God. Without prayer, we have no relationship with God, because we are cut off from God like the branch of a tree that is cut off, withers, and dies. But through prayer our sonship is established.

Sometimes the material problem drives us into deeper prayer. That is all right as long as we know that we are not praying to get a physical healing or a new automobile from God. We are going into prayer to receive the word of God, and when we receive It, It is fulfillment. Then, if our need is a physical healing, that is the way the Word appears. If our need is an automobile, that is the way It appears. If our need is a hotel room, that is the way God appears. But we dare not say, "God, I am going to need a hotel room." No! If we need a room in a hotel, however, we can turn to God and say, "God, let me hear Thy word. Give me the assurance of Thy presence." The moment we receive the assurance of that Presence, be assured there will be a room somewhere. Of course, we are not permitted to decide that it must be in some particular hotel, or even that it must be a hotel. Somehow our need will be fulfilled, be assured of that, at the level of the need.

When we put aside all this "Give me! Give me! Give me!" "Send me! Send me! Send me!" and live in our relationship with God, letting God's will be fulfilled in us, letting God's spiritual gifts reach us, we are fulfilled. But we do not receive the things we prayed for because those things are unknown to God, just as the things we really need are unknown to us in our human estate.

Prayer Is Living Through God

Prayer, then, is a way of life, living through God so that God's way may be fulfilled in us. This is a complete turning away from the earthly problem, the earthly sense of need, a complete turning within to a spiritual universe, seeking only spiritual Grace, spiritual harmony, spiritual peace, spiritual abundance.

"The effectual fervent prayer of a righteous man availeth much."[6] And what is that prayer? Trusting Omniscience, resting in Omnipotence, dwelling in Omnipresence, and always listening. Live the life of prayer so sacredly and so secretly that no man will ever draw any word of the great pearl you have found across your lips, but will, by observing the nature of your life, know that you have found it, that you tabernacle with God, that you commune with God within you. This wisdom is yours to keep, yours to live, yours with which to bless.

List of Scriptural References

1. *True Prayer, the Source of Our Good*

1. Romans 8:26.
2. I Kings 19:12.
3. Psalm 19:1.
4. Matthew 19:17.
5. John 10:30.
6. Matthew 19:6.
7. John 18:36.
8. John 14:27.
9. Philippians 2:5.

2. *Creating a Vacuum for the Inflow of the Spirit*

1. Psalm 23:1, 2.
2. Psalm 91:1.
3. Matthew 26:39.
4. I Kings 19:12.
5. I Samuel 3:9.
6. I Corinthians 3:16.
7. Luke 17:21.
8. Luke 4:18.

3. *Bringing Our Gift to the Altar*

1. I Kings 19:12.
2. John 14:27.
3. I Corinthians 3:16.
4. Hebrews 4:12.
5. Ephesians 5:14.
6. Psalm 19:14.
7. Matthew 25:40, 45.
8. John 12:32.
9. John 12:45.

4. *This Is Immortality*

1. John 10:10.
2. John 8:58.
3. John 10:30.
4. I Kings 19:12.
5. Romans 8:38, 39.
6. Galatians 2:20.

5. *God Is Omnipotent*

1. II Corinthians 3:17.
2. I Kings 19:12.
3. Matthew 6:27.
4. Matthew 9:6.
5. Matthew 5:39.
6. Matthew 26:52.
7. Psalm 46:10.
8. Matthew 24:44.

6. *Pray Without Ceasing*

1. Zechariah 4:6.
2. Isaiah 26:3.
3. Proverbs 3:5, 6.
4. I Thessalonians 5:17.
5. Psalm 91:1.
6. Job 23:14.
7. Psalm 138:8.
8. I John 4:4.
9. John 5:30.
10. John 8:58.
11. Deuteronomy 33:27.
12. John 10:30.
13. Psalm 24:1.
14. Isaiah 45:2.
15. Psalm 127:1.
16. Hebrews 4:12.

7. *Planting and Cultivating the Seed*

1. Acts 17:28.
2. I Corinthians 2:14.
3. Matthew 6:19.
4. Job 42:5.

8. *Let the Spirit Bear Witness*

1. Luke 4:18.
2. Romans 8:7.
3. Ezekiel 21:27.
4. Matthew 5:39.
5. Isaiah 45:2.

9. *Two or More Gathered Together*

1. Matthew 18:20.
2. I Corinthians 3:16.
3. John 10:30.
4. John 5:30.
5. John 5:31.
6. Luke 4:18.
7. Philippians 2:5.
8. Philippians 4:7.
9. Isaiah 1:18.
10. John 16:33.
11. Matthew 11:28.
12. John 14:27.

10. *The Widening Circle of Prayer*

1. Luke 17:21.
2. Matthew 13:46.

11. *Individuality Revealed Through Prayer*

1. II Corinthians 12:9.
2. Luke 15:31.
3. Genesis 1:1.
4. I Kings 19:12.
5. Job 26:7.
6. John 10:10.
7. Psalm 23:4.

12. *Living by Prayer*

1. I Kings 19:12.
2. John 18:36.
3. John 9:25.

4. John 12:45.
5. John 14:6.
6. James 5:16.

75 76 77 78 79 10 9 8 7 6 5 4 3 2 1